Straight
to the
Heart
of Zen

Straight

Eleven

Classic

Koans

and Their

Inner

Meanings

to the Heart

of Zen

PHILIP KAPLEAU

Edited by Rafe Martin

SHAMBHALA
Boston & London
2001

SHAMBHALA PUBLICATIONS, INC.
Horticultural Hall
300 Massachusetts Avenue
Boston, Massachusetts 02115
www.shambhala.com

Printed in the United States of America
⊗ This edition is printed on acid-free paper that meets
the American National Standards Institute z39.48 Standard.
Distributed in the United States by Random House, Inc.,
and in Canada by Random House of Canada Ltd

LIBRARY OF CONGRESS CATALOGING-IN-PUBLICATION DATA
Kapleau, Philip, 1912–
    Straight to the heart of Zen: eleven classic koans and their inner meanings/
Philip Kapleau.—
        p.   cm.
    Includes bibliographical references and index.
    ISBN 978-1-57062-593-0 (pbk.)
    1. Koan.   I. Title.
BQ9289.5 .K36   2001
294.3'84—dc21
00-067963

Contents

Preface

THIS COLLECTION of previously unpublished Zen talks (teishos) by the noted senior American Zen teacher Roshi Philip Kapleau—one of the true pioneers of Zen in the West and author of the classic *Three Pillars of Zen*—focuses on koans and fundamental issues of the spiritual life (which is, as Roshi Kapleau emphasizes, no different from our own ordinary daily existence). The talks in this collection come directly from the training hall, or *zendo*, and from the intense form of practice known as *sesshin* (Japanese for "to touch the mind"). As such, it is the first book to afford readers access to Roshi Kapleau's Zen, rather than to his more general teachings and talks about Zen that have been published in the past. For teishos, especially those on koans, are more than Zen "talks." They are direct presentations of the teacher's understanding of the Way.

While koans may be said to be uniquely Zen, in Roshi Kapleau's teishos they become as familiar, Western, and relevant as the questions that rouse us late at night from sleep: Why was I born? Why must I die? Why is there suffering? The confusions, doubts, despairs, and triumphs common to us all are the spiritual path. Koans are us, so to speak. Or, as Roshi Kapleau has often said, "Zen is not an esoteric teaching but one that is grounded and ordinary in the deepest sense."

Straight to the Heart of Zen is arranged in three main sections. As Zen begins with the Buddha's life and enlightenment, the first section explores three teishos, each on a koan drawn from an incident in the life of the Buddha.

Zen in the West, at least so far, is primarily a lay movement.

There is inspiration within the tradition for this, and the second section presents commentaries on three koans drawn from the lives of the three great lay figures of Zen—Vimalakirti of ancient India and Fu Daishi and Layman P'ang of ancient China.

The third section contains five teishos on koans that reflect fundamental concerns common to all of us, man or woman, monastic or lay, Buddhist or otherwise: Where is the road to nirvana, and how do I get on it? What will happen to me when I die? After enlightenment, what then?

The teishos have been arranged to suggest something of the path of maturing practice. From an initial meeting with a person of the Way (Goso's "No Words or Silence"), we face our deepest anxieties about life and death ("Dogo Expresses Condolences") and transcend the "Three Barriers" of Tosotsu, whose profound challenge must be faced by all Zen students before their training can be complete. We move on at last as mature practitioners capable of presenting the Way ourselves ("Kicking Over the Pitcher"), and, when we close the book, we find the Way extending beneath our own feet ("Kempo's One Way").

Roshi Kapleau is now in his late eighties and fully retired. But his inspiring voice can still be found in these talks, tirelessly bringing home the truth that has always been before us. As the verse to case number thirty of the *Mumonkan*, or *Gateless Barrier*, one of the primary collections of koans, puts it, "Under a blue sky in bright sunlight one need not search around asking what is Buddha. This is like hiding loot in one's pocket and declaring oneself innocent."

Still, without the guidance of an awakened teacher, how would we ever really know this? The words and actions of such teachers, going all the way back to the Buddha himself, are the living heart of Zen.

Rafe Martin
April 2000

Acknowledgments

AT EIGHTY-EIGHT, my current age, I don't foresee doing many more books. For this one I was glad to have the help of good friends. Polly Young-Eisendrath stimulated my initial interest in doing yet one more book. Longtime friend and disciple Rafe Martin took on the lion's share of the work by helping select teishos, listening to hours of tapes and then editing these oral talks into readable texts, and also by suggesting themes for the book as a whole. Zen teacher, disciple, and longtime friend Lawson Sachter carefully reviewed each written teisho with an eye to the lineage of my teaching. Bodhin Kjolhede, Abbot of the Zen Center, graciously took time from his demanding schedule to look over the entire manuscript with a discerning eye and suggest important refinements and clarifications. Jeannine Schumacher helped by transcribing most of these teishos from archived audiotape into rough text. Marion Taylor took up the task of acquiring needed permissions and creating the bibliography, as well as helping with the glossary. My heartfelt thanks to all.

Philip Kapleau
April 2000

Straight

to the

Heart

of Zen

Introduction

THESE TEISHOS, or Zen presentations of the dharma, have been selected from recordings made over the last twenty-five years or so in
the zendo of the Rochester (New York) Zen Center. Most were originally presented at sesshin, or Zen retreats. Except for daily teisho
and *dokusan*—the one-to-one meeting of student and teacher—sesshin
are essentially conducted in silence over a period of anywhere from
one or two to seven days. The practice of sesshin is said to have origi-
nated with the rainy-season retreats of the monks in the Buddha's
own time, twenty-five hundred years ago in India, and it remains at
the core of Zen training today.

These particular teishos of mine have never been put into written
form before and have never been heard by anyone except the fifty or
so participants who happened to be attending the particular sesshin
in which each was given. Each of these teishos is on a koan.

Much has already been written on koans, yet there remains misun-
derstanding and confusion as to what koans actually are. In essence,
koans are a form of spiritual practice unique to Zen. Since the days of
the great Zen masters of ancient China, they have been used to help
Zen students realize, refine, and embody the Buddha's teachings. Literally they are often baffling verbal expressions, puzzling or frustrating to logic, built around or taken from the sayings and doings of the
ancient Zen masters, or occasionally from mythic/historical events in
the life of the Buddha. Several books of koans, collections put together during the great T'ang era, are in regular use in Zen training
centers today, the two most central being the *Mumonkan*, or *Gateless*

Barrier, and the *Hekiganroku*, or *Blue Cliff* (sometimes translated as *Blue Rock*) *Record*.

Koans are not intellectual puzzles or conundrums, nor are they tricky and clever; rather, they are direct and profound. Every koan points to our True Face and True Home, which is why every teisho is a vivid presentation of truth itself, not simply a talk about it. To realize the essence of a koan is to realize the primal condition of one's own mind—a state of awareness, freedom, wisdom, and compassion. Viewed from this innate condition of Being, a koan is the clearest formulation of an essential truth—the truth of one's own nature. In essence, koans are tools designed by the spiritual geniuses of ancient China to help us realize the truth of our own nature and the nature of all living things, and to do so in the midst of our ordinary lives.

Working on koans under the guidance of an awakened and disciplined teacher is a concrete way of bringing to life the four bodhisattva vows chanted daily in all Zen centers, zendos, and monasteries:

All beings without number I vow to liberate.
Endless blind passions I vow to uproot.
Dharma gates beyond measure I vow to penetrate.
The great way of Buddha I vow to attain.

It is a tried and true way to awaken one's own sleeping buddha heart and mind and to liberate them to work for the welfare of others. The heart of Zen is not a mechanical pump. It is a roaring lion, and it is radiant.

The teishos in this collection have not been arranged in any formal progression, as from easy to hard, simple to complex, or earlier masters to later ones. Yet there is a rhythm and structure to the book as a whole, which is to bring us from the life of the Buddha, through the lives of the great lay figures of the past, to fundamental issues of our own ordinary daily lives and the path of our own maturing practice. These last, which emphasize that our own ordinary life and concerns are the Buddha Way, focus on essential questions: What is the way to enlightenment? What is Buddha? How do I get on the path?

Is speech or silence closer to the truth? What if I feel inadequate—does that bar me from practice? What is life? What is death?

All truth-seekers must, in one way or another, at one time or another, face these concerns. Lest we think that we today are alone with such issues, these koans make it clear that they were already being squarely dealt with by the enlightened teachers of ancient China long ago.

Not everyone practicing Zen necessarily finds koan training to be his or her best mode of practice. Some people work on koans for a while and then choose to work on one fundamental question or do *shikantaza*, the practice of pure attention. Most practitioners start with breath-counting or following the breath and begin koan training or *shikantaza* later. There is no set path. Still, as koans reveal so much of Zen tradition and its uniquely creative style, dynamic spirit, and profound wisdom, commentaries on them can benefit anyone with a genuine interest in spiritual practice.

Actually everything, just as it is, is a koan, the expression of perfection. To realize this perfection is the working out of a living koan. All koans—and there are many of them—express this perfection in different forms, but all of them reveal the essential perfection of existence lying beyond the realm of ever-changing appearances. Every koan points to our Original Mind and is designed to bring us to the realization of it. You could say that all koans have a fundamental purpose—to lead us to our own real home, the one we knew before our parents gave birth to us.

In his book *Philosophies of India*, Heinrich Zimmer, Joseph Campbell's teacher, makes an observation that fits koans perfectly. "Knowledge," he said, "is the reward of action. . . . For it is by doing things that one becomes transformed. Executing a symbolical gesture, actually living through, to the very limit, a particular role, one comes to realize the truth inherent in the role. Suffering its consequences, one fathoms and exhausts its contents."[1]

And Shibayama-roshi, in his fine book *Zen Comments on the Mumonkan*, has this to say:

Koan are originally sayings or doings in the form of mondo [dharma exchanges], instructions, talks, etc., left by great Zen masters. In other words, drawing on their deep Zen experiences, they freely expressed their Zen under different circumstances. The significance of koan varies greatly one from another, and they cannot be classified by any forms or rules. Some may encourage training; some may be mondo between two people to test closely and refine each other; some may express profound and lucid spirituality; some may stress the truth of equality, or the working aspect of the Truth in differentiation; some may emphasize the truth that "one is all; all is one"; some may wipe off all the stinks and even smacks of Zen; some may not fit under any category. . . . Once my own teacher explained the role of koan in Zen training . . . : "Needless to say, the task or role of the koan is to help a student open his Zen eye, to deepen his Zen attainment, and to refine his Zen personality. It is a means in Zen training, but in actual practice the koan does not lead a student along an easy and smooth shortcut, like other ordinary means. . . . The . . . koan will mercilessly take away all our intellect and knowledge."[2]

As it is our fierce attachment to our intellect and knowledge that blinds us to the greater truth, this seeming mercilessness is really a great mercy. "Taking away" means taking away attachment and liberating us from bondage. It is not that we are left without intellect and knowledge. Far from it. It is just that we are no longer left at their mercy.

PART ONE

Koans

of the

Buddha

1

The Buddha Holds Up
a Flower

THE GATELESS BARRIER, CASE 6

Once when the World-Honored One in ancient times was upon Vulture Peak [Mount Grdrakuta], he held up a flower before the assembly of monks. At this time all were silent. The Venerable Kashyapa alone broke into a smile. The World-Honored One said, "I have the All-Pervading Eye of the True Dharma, the Secret Heart of Incomparable Nirvana, the True Aspect of Formless Form. It does not rely on letters and is transmitted outside the scriptures. I now pass it on to Mahakashyapa."

COMMENTARY

Golden-faced Kudon impudently forced the good people into depravity. Advertising sheep's heads, he sells dog flesh, but with some genius. However, supposing that at that time all the monks had laughed. How would the "All-including eye of the True Dharma" have been handed on? Or if Kashyapa had not smiled, how would the True Dharma have been transmitted? If you say that the True Dharma can be handed on [anyway], the golden-faced old man with his loud voice deceived the simple villagers. If you say it can't be transmitted, why did Buddha say he had handed it on to Kashyapa?

VERSE

> Holding up a flower,
> The tail is revealed.
> Kashyapa smiles,
> The monks don't know what to do.

Kashyapa is *Maha* ("great") Kashyapa, one of the chief disciples of the Buddha. He was also one of the oldest of the Buddha's followers and was said to have been a distant cousin of the Buddha. After the Buddha's *parinirvana*, or entrance into nirvana at the time of death, it was he who was selected to lead the community of Buddhist practitioners, or *sangha*. Obviously he was a man of superlative wisdom and ability.

When we say "the Buddha," of course, we are talking about the historical person whose personal name was Siddhartha and whose family name was Gautama. He was also called Shakyamuni, which means "the silent sage of the Shakyas," the Shakyas being his family clan. Shakyamuni Buddha was born around the year 563 BCE in the foothills of what is present-day Nepal. His father was the ruler of a small principality, somewhat like Monaco today.

The Sanskrit word *buddha* is actually a title meaning "awakened." It comes from the root word *buddh*, meaning "absolute truth" or "ultimate mind." Perhaps in English it has some distant etymological relation to "bud," or to "flower" into Truth. One who has achieved this is a "budded one," a buddha. So, a buddha is one who has attained this absolute state, who has experienced, or has awakened to, Absolute Mind, or ultimate truth. He or she is a matured human being, one who has flowered into full potential. Often in Buddhism a lotus flower—which rises up out of the mud, climbs through the murky water toward the dim light above, and at last fully blossoms in the blazing sunlight—is a visual metaphor for this entire process of inner spiritual growth. A buddha is a flowered being, one whose mind has fully opened. Of course, there are infinite degrees of such opening. Someone who has had a first kensho has attained a brief glimpse into Truth. Full enlightenment and complete buddhahood still lie far ahead.

Most people are familiar with the broad outlines of the Buddha's life: he married at the age of sixteen and later had a son. Deeply troubled by the sorrows and the tribulations of human life, he could no longer endure the luxury and comfort of his father's palace. And so one night, at the age of twenty-nine, he left his wife and young child and became a wandering ascetic. For the next six years he practiced the most painful austerities possible, earnestly seeking enlightenment. When he was at the point of death he realized he could not come to awakening if he lost this human body. So he gave up the ascetic path and decided to steer a middle course between asceticism and self-indulgence, attaining the "middle way" of zazen. After doing ardent zazen all through the night under the bodhi tree, he had a great awakening when he happened to glance up at the planet Venus shining brightly in the dawn sky. What he said at that moment has been recorded in various sutras. In the Mahayana tradition's *Avatamsaka-sutra* it is recorded that he spontaneously exclaimed something like this—Wonder of wonders! All beings, whether male or female, tall or short, black or white, ugly or beautiful have this all-embracing bodhi-nature. All are buddhas! But because their minds are turned upside-down through delusive thinking, they fail to realize Self-nature, and therefore they suffer.

Later his son became one of his close disciples and his wife became a nun in the order that developed around him and his teachings after that historic spiritual event. After his great enlightenment, Siddhartha Gautama, the ex-prince who was now known as the Buddha, the Enlightened One, tirelessly taught the dharma—that is, the truth of the universe—always suiting his teaching to the capacity of his hearers' understanding. This has become a fundamental principle in Buddhism: the teaching must be suited to the capacity of the person to understand. For the next forty-five years until the age of eighty and his death, or entrance into parinirvana, he continued traveling the dusty roads of India, compassionately teaching whoever came before him, wherever he went.

So much for the two protagonists of this koan. Let us now return to the case itself. "Once when the World-Honored One in ancient times was upon Vulture Peak, he held up a flower before the assembly of monks." The "World-Honored One" is, of course, an appellation of the Buddha, and a beautiful one. Mount Grdrakuta was also known as Eagle or Vulture Peak, because its top resembled the head of a great bird. "He held up a flower before the assembly of monks." The literal accuracy of the incident that forms the ground of the koan is doubted by historians. Whether it ever happened or whether it happened exactly as recorded has nothing at all to do with the truth of Zen. The beginnings of all vital religions are shrouded in myth and legend. We must never make the mistake of thinking that a myth or a legend is a story that's untrue. Rather, it's a story so majestic, so all-encompassing, that it can't be kept within the small compass of fact. The truth of Zen does not depend upon whether this story is or is not literally, historically true. Since it so beautifully illustrates Zen principles, we accept it as being true in the profoundest sense.

The Buddha "held up a flower before the assembly of monks." When you stop to think of it, there's really nothing more expressive of the purity, innocence, and all-encompassing quality of our True Mind than a flower. A flower has an innate, inner vitality, a single-minded determination to face the sun, to grow, and finally to fully blossom, as well as to serve: bees are given pollen, animals eat the blossoms, humans find beauty. At the same time, it does not assert itself in any way. When the time comes to wither, flowers simply drop their petals, dry up, crumple, and are gone. The lotus flower, as has been mentioned, is itself an ancient Buddhist symbol of spiritual unfolding. The natural world and the truths of Mind reflect each other endlessly.

There's a poem titled "Flowers" that we use in memorial services:

Such a solemn world of flowers!
Such a spectacle,
this rich world of the flowers!
All beings are living brightness
fulfilled with brightness
on the earth, under the heavens.

There is no gap between matter and man,
between sentient and nonsentient being:
all are living, all are dancing—
slate and pebbles are whispering,
dust and trash are shouting,
trees and grasses speak, the land sings.

People are born out of the earth.
The world appears
in the pores of each one's skin.
Gods appear from all beings.
Unimaginable light shines out!
Out of one pore appear
ten thousand times
ten thousand universes.
At the very point of this moment
is a bursting forth of the eternal Buddha.
One Buddha has the world, and holds all
universes. Each universe holds
ten thousand times
ten thousand universes.

The world is a flower.
Gods are flowers.
Enlightened ones are flowers.
All phenomena are flowers.
Red flowers, white flowers, green flowers,
yellow flowers, black flowers,

all of the different kinds
of the colors of flowers,
all of the different kinds
of love's shining-forth.

Life unfolds from life and returns into life.
Such an immense universe! Oh, many lives!
Flowers of gratitude, flowers of sorrow,
flowers of suffering, flowers of joy,
laughter's flowers, anger's flowers,
heaven's flowers, hell's flowers.
Each connected to the others
and each making the others grow.

When our real Mind's Eye
opens this world of flowers,
all beings shine,
music echoes through mountains and oceans.
One's world becomes the world of millions.
The individual becomes the human race.
All lives become the individual—
billions of mirrors
all reflecting each other.

There is death and life,
there is no death, no life.
There is changing life, there is unchanging life.
There is nirvana, there is samsara.
Clouds change into multitudinous forms.
Water changes form as it wishes,
taking the shape of its container.
Flowers change color, moment by moment.

Such a vivid world! Such a bright you!
You were born out of these flowers,

you gave birth to these flowers.
You have no beginning and no ending,
you are bottomless and limitless,
even as also you are infinitesimal dust.
You are the flower.

You become man and embrace all women,
you become woman and embrace all men.
You are love,
you are the flower.
All beings shine out of their uniqueness,
all melt into the oneness of colors.
You are one, you are many,
only one moment, only one unique place,
only the unique you.
Beside you there is nothing:
you dance, appearing in all.

Sitting in silence, dancing in gratitude,
dancing like the huge waves,
moving like the white clouds,
you see you, you see the you who sees you.
With gratitude you see,
with gratitude you are seen:
the world as you, you as you;
you as actor, you as audience;
you as subject, you as object.
You are free. You are not free.

From nowhere you came. You go nowhere.
You stay nowhere. You are nowhere attached.
You occupy everything, you occupy nothing.
You are the becoming of indescribable change.
You are love. You are the flower.[1]

One day the Buddha was seated before an immense crowd of those who had come to hear his spiritual discourse. But instead of speaking, he held up a flower and said not a word. All were silent, stunned, puzzled. Only the venerable Mahakashyapa smiled. Why were all silent? Why did the venerable Kashyapa alone break into a smile? Among this assembly were many enlightened practitioners. Didn't they understand what the Buddha was doing? This is one of the questions of this koan, one of the barriers. Also, if the Venerable Kashyapa smiled, what was he conveying by this smile? What was the Buddha conveying when he held up this single flower? You must grasp all this if you want to grasp the essence of this koan. Was it a case of a flower speaking to a flower? Were Kashyapa and the Buddha a special kind of flower and the monks another? If we are all flowers, why did the others fail to smile?

The koan goes on: "The World-Honored One said, 'I have the All-Pervading Eye of the True Dharma, the Secret Heart of Incomparable Nirvana, the True Aspect of Formless Form.' " Shibayama-roshi says, "True Dharma is the Dharma of as-it-isness, where not even a thought of consciousness is working. It is 'it,' or the Truth that transcends space and time."[2] The dharma is also that which is in space and time. It is the law of constant change. All things are being born, growing, flourishing, blossoming, withering, decaying, and dying. Looked at from the point of view of impermanence, there is nothing but change and transformation. To paraphrase Zen Master Dogen, the impermanence of things is buddha-nature.

Simultaneously, looked at from the side of unchangeableness, the Absolute, there is only *This*, boundless, limitless, beyond all change, beyond all definitions and conditions. Shibayama-roshi continues, "All-pervading means it is the source of creativity and wonderful working which is absolutely free, perfect, inexhaustible, and infinite. Incomparable Nirvana," he says, "is the never born, never dying Reality itself. It is the subjectivity that freely expresses itself and works under all different situations."[3]

The term *nirvana* is old and is considered so quaint in Japanese Zen as to be almost obsolete. Yet it's very useful, and it remains one of those beautiful Sanskrit words that can suggest a broad meaning. At the same time, it's a word that has caused a great deal of trouble. Years ago early translators of Sanskrit, many of whom were not Buddhists at all, used the word in a negative way. Since the root meaning of nirvana is "to blow out, to extinguish," they took it to mean that one becomes a kind of a nothing. Well, it is a nothing, but a Nothing that's an Everything. And of course to blow out, or to extinguish, means to extinguish our mind of ego, of our deforming passions, so that our true, unlimited Mind, the Mind which is not born and so never dies, may come into consciousness. Nirvana is a state of absolute freedom, without restriction. A consummation devoutly to be wished, as Hamlet puts it.

To go on: In speaking of "the Secret Heart of . . . Formless Form," Shibayama-roshi comments, "A form takes a shape and shows discrimination. When there is no discrimination there is no form, and this formless form is the true form of Reality, for it is the self-manifestation of 'Mu.' "[4] The succinct *Prajnaparamita-sutra*, which is chanted daily in Zen centers and temples worldwide, states, "Form is only emptiness, emptiness only form"—one of the most famous dictums of Zen. If we try to separate form from emptiness, we are in trouble and fall at once into duality. We cannot take an apple, for example, or a chair and say, This part is the formlessness and this part is the form. Can we split the unsplittable?

The basis of Zen is the formless True Mind, our formless Self. Since it has no form, it is capable of assuming all forms at all times in response to conditions and circumstances. There's a wonderful verse to koan number twenty in the *Mumonkan*, "A Man of Great Strength," that speaks of this Mind, saying, "Lifting his leg he kicks up the scented ocean, lowering his head, he looks down upon the four Dhyana Heavens. His body is so big there's nowhere to put it. Please finish this verse yourself."

Dhyana refers to meditation. The implication is that these are the highest, purest heavens. Here is the mysterious dharma gate: the formless form, the incomparable nirvana, the all-pervading eye of truth, as our present koan has it. And its transmission does not rely on the written words and letters of the various Buddhist scriptures, but on personal experience—outside all written texts, no matter how profound. However, "transmitted outside the scriptures" doesn't mean that the sutras, the recorded classical teachings of the Buddha, are useless. Far from it. Reading the sutras can deepen our faith and refine our understanding. Sometimes such reading can startle the mind into opening to a new perspective. But it takes a living being to breathe life into the sutras, for they are the encoded spirit of the Buddha. It's like a musical recording. The music is there, but it takes a record player and electricity to bring it out. This is exactly the way it is with the sutras. And that player, that record, that electricity are one's own Mind, one's own enlightenment. My teacher, Yasutani-roshi, emphasized that all of Buddhist philosophy, doctrine, and teaching come out of the Buddha's enlightenment. Without the Buddha's enlightenment, there would be no philosophy and no doctrine.

This is why in Zen, especially, the emphasis tends to be on the Buddha's enlightenment, not on the facts or the legends of his life. This doesn't exclude them. Indeed, all such details of the Buddha's life add tremendous resonance to our own life path and our own exertions. But the primary emphasis is on his experience, for it is this experience that gives *life* to the Buddha's life. Otherwise, his life is merely history—the account of what a certain man said and did many years ago.

The Buddha says, "It does not rely on letters and is transmitted outside the scriptures. I now pass it on to Mahakashyapa." Can what is beyond all letters and all teaching be passed on? Is it something tangible and concrete that can be handed from one to another? Is it something in time and space? And who passes what to whom? Who is there to pass it and who to receive? "Transmission of the dharma" seems like a rather cool, abstract, and almost mechanical expression, like something moving inexorably along a super conveyor belt. It is not. In Zen, the transmission from teacher to student-disciple is the heart's blood of the tradition. It is intimate, deeply personal, and profound.

Is such transmission, beginning with the Buddha and passing on to Mahakashyapa and then from him on to all the others in India, China, Japan, and now the West, just a myth—in the most limited sense of the word, a fable? No, it is not. What this expression means is that when the student's mind is in complete accord with the teacher's, there is transmission. Nothing passes over, and yet they are absolutely one. This complete identity is transmission. Complete understanding.

"Golden-faced Kudon impudently forced the good people into depravity." *Golden-faced Kudon* is an appellation for the Buddha. *Golden-faced* refers to the historical fact that his skin was probably a light golden-brown color, but it also undoubtedly suggests the radiance of his face—and not only his face, but his whole being. Mumon, in his usual tongue-in-cheek manner, says the Buddha "impudently forced the good people into depravity. Advertising sheep's heads, he sells dog flesh, but with some genius."

What is this? We can well imagine the surprise of the monks when the Buddha, instead of giving his usual lofty dharma-talk, just holds up a flower—twirls it, perhaps, in his hand, and looks at it. The many believers have come to hear an edifying, spiritually illuminating talk. Their minds are composed. They are sitting quietly, ready to be lifted out of their daily confusions and troubles by the Buddha's inspiring words. Instead, all he does is hold up a flower. No words are spoken. There is only a flower and a smile. Doubtless many are surprised. Many others are disappointed and bewildered. A few, perhaps just one, smiles. A smile that flowers, a flower that smiles.

Mumon adds: "Supposing that at the time, all the monks had laughed. How would the 'All-including eye of the True Dharma' have been handed on?" Don't all people have the buddha-nature? Isn't that what the sutras tell us? Don't they say that all people, all beings, even, are fully endowed with buddha-nature and are intrinsically buddhas? Aren't all people flowers in the sense that we read in the poem? Aren't they lotuses about to bloom? Why, then, does he select

Mahakashyapa alone of all of those gathered expectantly there? Is he playing favorites? Is it fair?

As Mumon says, suppose at the time everyone had laughed or smiled. Then what? Would the Buddha have been in a dilemma? Would he have had to hand down transmission to all of them? Then again, didn't many of them already have transmission by virtue of their own confirmed enlightenment?

"Or if Kashyapa had not smiled, how would the True Dharma have been transmitted?" And to whom? Do you see how thorough-going old Mumon is? Working on this koan, how would you demonstrate it? You can't explain. You can't say, Well, I think . . . and hope for the best. You have to really answer! But you wouldn't necessarily need words.

Then Mumon goes on to say, "If you say that the True Dharma can be handed on, the golden-faced old man with his loud voice deceived the simple villagers." Mumon is saying that if you hold to that view, why, you're no better than the Buddha. You're just as much of a faker as he is, saying that there is something to pass on. What would it mean to be just as much of a faker as the Buddha? In any case, is that a good or bad thing? He continues, "If you say it can't be transmitted, why did Buddha say he had handed it on to Kashyapa?"

Mumon, ever the resolute Zen master, puts us into an irresolvable intellectual dilemma. His "madness" is his method. His hope, as a true teacher, is that we may use that dilemma to go beyond it. He wants us to realize the reality that lies behind all the twists and turns of logic and reason. Mumon is rubbing our noses in our deeply held attachments to logic and reason. We turn to these tools at every opportunity, yet should we? You think they are so useful, he is saying. Well, let's see if they can help you find your way out of this! Many may find these tactics terribly frustrating. There is no need to bemoan your fate; even as great a master as Hakuin spoke passionately of those "vile and poisonous koans." He too knew the agony of facing the limits of the intellect and of having to go beyond it.

Shibayama-roshi responds with an old saying: "The father stole the sheep and the son acknowledged it."[5] The Buddha stole a march on all the monks, and only Mahakashyapa acknowledged it—that is, he alone knew what the Buddha was up to. Certainly the implication is one of profound intimacy. The father knows the child, and the child knows the father. But what's this about stealing a sheep? Isn't that dishonest? In any event, how did the Buddha steal a sheep just by holding up a flower and twirling it in his fingers? There's only one way to know. If you want to understand, you'll have to become the flower itself. Then there is no Buddha, there is no Mahakashyapa, there is no self. There is just a flower that smiles, evoking a smile that flowers.

Shibayama-roshi quotes a mondo (a dharma encounter that can lead to an experience of Truth) in which a disciple asked a Zen master, whose name was Ungo, this question: "It is said that the World-Honored One gave a secret talk of holding up a flower, and Kasho [Kashyapa] by smiling did not conceal it. What does this mean?" This disciple, by the way, was a governor, an important man and one with experience in Zen.

Ungo called out, "Oh, Governor." "Yes, Master," replied the governor. "Do you understand?" asked the master. When the governor answered, "No, I do not," Ungo told him, "If you do not understand, it shows that the World-Honored One did make the secret talk. If you do understand, it means that Kasho [Kashyapa] did not conceal it."[6]

That's a very interesting mondo on this koan. Do you understand? Zen Master Hakuin has a teisho on this koan. He says,

Everybody, male or female, without exception, has the True Dharma. Still, Shakyamuni expressly declared that he had handed it to Kasho alone. He is certainly deceiving people. Yet I won't say that there was no transmission taking place. I now hold up my hosou [whisk] like this, the truth of which no dull, ordinary monks can ever grasp. Kasho grasped it, so he smiled. There will not be too many who can fully appreciate the real significance of this smile. When one gets it, there is the true transmission.[7]

It is no different, really, from any of the other koans. Everyone re-
ceives transmission who comprehends this. Everyone is a Mahakashyapa. Everyone is a Shakyamuni Buddha. Comprehension is all.

The verse says:

Holding up a flower,
The tail is revealed.

If a snake is trying to hide itself and if just the tiniest tip of its tail is
showing, it may think that it has adequately concealed itself, but it
has also really revealed itself completely. Or a child covers its own
head with a blanket and thinks it is hidden. The enlightened mind is
an open secret. Everybody has it. Everybody in their heart of hearts
knows, has had a glimpse, even if it's the barest glimpse. Everyone
has resided in complete peace at some moment, for at least one swift,
timeless second of absolute oneness and self-forgetfulness. In the secret heart of everyone there is that secret of secrets. But as one becomes attached to name and fame and form, to the ways of the world
and the joyless pursuit of pleasure, to the chase after prestige, money,
and power, the wonderful secret gets lost. And now the Buddha has
revealed it openly with a flower. This flower is neither big nor small.
It is not yellow, blue, or green. It is indestructible. It is always
blooming, alive and fresh until, alas, our mind becomes clouded over
with the dirts of ego. Then it's just as though we've taken the sunlight out of the flower and it begins to wilt. Yet while it may wilt,
it is never destroyed. Given the right circumstances, it will bloom
again and continue to bloom.

Kashyapa smiles,
The monks don't know what to do.

There are people who find it difficult to smile. Somehow their faces
have become almost frozen, and when they do smile, you can almost
hear a loud *crack!* Perhaps people who have difficulty in smiling
should practice smiling the smile of Mahakashyapa, the Buddha's "ar-

chaic smile," which allows the warmth of one's heart to flow out. This can have a very beneficial effect, not only cosmetically but spiritually. A smile blossoms, evoking smiles that flower in their turn. All the springtime, all blossoming and budding is in such a smile. Smiling is something everyone can do, monk or layperson, man or woman, young or old. If even a baby can do it, how hard can it be? How complex? The transformation of a face through the play of a smile upon it, just a faint little smile, is really a beautiful thing. This koan is not only about a flower but also about a smile.

Why? Don't come up with reasons and answers. None will do. Do you understand? If you do not, it means that there is indeed a secret teaching. What is it? If you do understand, it means it is not concealed. How will you present it? Where will you look for your answers? Once the Buddha held up a flower. Why not look there?

2

A Woman Comes Out
of Meditation

THE GATELESS BARRIER, CASE 42

Once in ancient times the World-Honored One came to the place where many buddhas were assembled. When Manjusri arrived there, the buddhas all returned to their original places. A single woman remained close to the Buddha's throne in deepest meditation. Manjusri said to the Buddha, "How is it that this woman can be so close to your throne and I cannot be?" The Buddha spoke to Manjusri, saying, "You may awaken this woman from her deep meditation and ask her yourself how this can be." Manjusri walked around her three times, snapped his fingers once, took her up to the Brahma heaven and tried all his supernatural powers, but he could not bring her out of her deep meditation. The World-Honored One said, "Even a hundred thousand Manjusris could not get her out of her concentrated condition. But down below, past one billion, two hundred million countries, as innumerable as the sands of the Ganges, there's a bodhisattva named Momyo, who will be able to awaken this woman from her profound meditation." Thereupon Momyo emerged out of the earth and bowed to the World-Honored One, who told him what he wanted him to do. Momyo then walked to the woman, snapped his fingers once, and at this she came out of her meditation.

COMMENTARY

The drama old Shakya puts on is a great hodgepodge. Just tell me now, Manjusri is the teacher of the seven buddhas—why couldn't he get the woman out of her samadhi, when Momyo, a beginner, could? If you can firmly grasp this point, then for you this busy life of ignorance and discrimination will be the life of the dragon samadhi [i.e., supreme satori].

VERSE

One could awaken her, the other could not;
Both have their own freedom.
A god mask and a devil mask;
The failure is wonderful indeed.

We seem to be breathing the exotic air of India here, rather than the typically down-to-earth Chinese atmosphere of the koans. At any minute one might almost expect some of these characters to begin levitating. Yet it is a wonderful, magically cosmic drama. How brilliantly the Chinese Zen Master Mumon has taken an incident from an Indian sutra and turned it into a koan, one that allows us to clarify *prajna* wisdom, which is quite different from mere philosophical teaching.

Fundamental, or prajna, wisdom can be equated with the world of Oneness, while philosophical understanding can be equated with the world of differentiation, the world of the "ten thousand things," as it is called. Simply put, the world of discrimination, or differentiation, is the ordinary world of pain, strife, and struggle. The undifferentiated world, the world of "no-thingness," is the world of enlightenment. But it may also be a state or condition in which one hasn't yet put one's awareness—realized through awakening—to work to help others. It's pure freedom, but a freedom that isn't doing any work. From a practical point of view, it's still half-baked.

Legend has it that Shakyamuni Buddha, after his supreme enlightenment, relished this great freedom and joy for three weeks and wondered whether he could actually go out into the world and teach. Could the world understand that there was really nothing to teach, no one to be taught, and no one to do the teaching? It was so profound—and so simple. In *kensho*, depending on how deep our realization is, we catch a glimpse of this world of emptiness. We awaken to our fundamental, or prajna, wisdom, but our insight isn't yet interfused with the world of discrimination, and, until it is, it is not really working. We might say that the discriminative aspect is the form of which the equality aspect is the content. According to one's karma, one's life can take many forms or expressions. The Japanese word for this is *go-en*. The Sanskrit word, now common in English, is *karma*. *Go-en* is a bit more precise. *Go* means action, doing, deeds and their consequences. And *en* means primary and secondary causes. For example, if a farmer plants certain crops, the primary cause is the planting of seeds, which turn into crops. But the secondary causes are the soil, the rain, the sunshine, and so forth.

This koan explores both aspects, fundamental wisdom or equality and differentiation. The koan says that in ancient times the World-Honored One came to a place where many buddhas were assembled. Even buddhas, it seems, have their conferences and meetings. Of course, what they are meeting about is how to help sentient beings be free of suffering. When Manjusri arrived, the buddhas all returned to their original places. In Buddhist iconography, Manjusri is traditionally on the Buddha's right, sitting on a magnificent golden lion, which represents the dignity, majesty, nobility, and power of our True Nature, True Mind. Often he carries in his right hand a delusion-cutting sword. Sometimes he holds a sutra in the other hand, usually a scroll of the *Prajnaparamita-sutra*, or *Heart of Perfect Wisdom*. His flower is the blue lotus. It is said that at one time he had been a buddha himself. Yet so great was his compassion that he descended once more into the world of bodhisattvas and became the teacher of the seven buddhas, one of whom is the buddha of our own historical period, Shakyamuni Buddha.

The number seven is really a way of indicating that there have been innumerable buddhas before Shakyamuni Buddha and there will be innumerable buddhas after Shakyamuni Buddha. Buddhas have their domains, their own worlds where they're in charge, acting as trustworthy guides to all beings. Buddhas have only one aim—to bring deluded, suffering beings to awakening. What do these beings awaken to? To the truth that they themselves have also always been buddhas!

Now why, when Manjusri, the great bodhisattva of wisdom, arrives, do all the buddhas return to their original places? And what are their original places? These are points that the koan asks us to clarify.

Oddly, it turns out that even after the buddhas returned to their original places, a woman remained in deep meditation near the Buddha's seat. In Asian countries, in ancient times (and in some countries even today), women were considered inferior. It is an old prejudice, and like all prejudices is baseless and so hurts us all. The implication is simply that someone who had no hierarchical position was seated where only a person of great merit should sit. It would be like a commoner walking into a throne room and sitting next to the king. So Manjusri, the greatly compassionate, wise, fully spiritually developed wisdom bodhisattva, is puzzled. And he asks, "How is it that this woman can be so close to your throne and I cannot be?"

We must see what the woman represents. We must understand what Manjusri represents. And we must see, too, why it is that Manjusri, who was the highly respected teacher of the seven buddhas, can't come close to the Buddha's seat.

It is very easy, if one is literal-minded, to get annoyed with all this. "What's going on here?" you might think. "I thought we were working on a koan that explores fundamental problems of life and death, my life and death. Instead we seem to be lost in a legendary, dramatic show." But this is part of the genius of the *Mumonkan*. If we

let ourselves get into the koan and don't get caught up in nonessentials, it becomes very interesting. We find ourselves getting deeper
into the koan by the very reason of its legendary, dramatic elements,
in which crucial points are embedded. It's like the later plays of
Shakespeare, whose magical imagery heightens the dramatic effect
and deepens our interest. There is the reverberation and resonance of
myth.

Now the Buddha speaks to Manjusri, saying, "You may awaken
this woman from her deep meditation and ask her yourself how this
can be." In other words: Find out yourself. What is the Buddha up
to? What does he want Manjusri to find out? And what exactly is
meditation? What is *samadhi*? The woman, after all, is said to be in
deepest samadhi.

So Manjusri walks around the woman three times, snaps his fingers once, takes her up to the Brahmin heaven, and tries all his supernatural powers. Yet he can't awaken her from her deep meditation.
He can't get an answer. He can't awaken her. Or can he? The Buddha
says that even if a hundred thousand Manjusris were to get together,
they could not awaken the woman from her deep meditation. Of
course, in one sense nobody can enter into the mind or the meditation
of another person. But what exactly does it mean to awaken her from
meditation? One would assume that if anybody could awaken her, it
would certainly be Manjusri, who was of the highest rank of all the
bodhisattvas. But no, he can't. Not even endless, countless, limitless
Manjusris can, says the Buddha.

Then the Buddha continues, "But down below, past one billion,
two hundred million countries, as innumerable as the sands of the
Ganges, there's a bodhisattva called Momyo, who will be able to
awaken this woman from her profound meditation." As soon as he
says this, Momyo emerges from the earth and makes a bow to the
World-Honored One, who orders him to awaken the woman.
Momyo walks to her, snaps his fingers once, and she quickly comes
out of meditation.

How is it that somebody like Momyo, who is no more than halfway along in the process of becoming a full bodhisattva, can awaken

her, while Manjusri cannot? There are said to be fifty-two stages to the bodhisattva's career, and Momyo is only part of the way there. Some sources say he is only a rank beginner. In either case, he's obviously nowhere near as spiritually developed as Manjusri. What is going on? How can someone much less spiritually developed accomplish what someone who is very spiritually developed cannot? Logic is thrown out the window. It makes no sense at all. We must get away from the words. We must read between the lines if we are to see what the Buddha in his great wisdom and compassion is trying to get us to see.

One of the great virtues of koans is they get us to think, not in an analytical way, but with our complete mind. We have to use all our intuitive powers and feel and act as well as think. All our faculties come into play when we're seriously working on a koan. The koan rouses and awakens us. The koan brings us to life as we bring it to life. As an old saying puts it, "The ancient teachings illumine the mind and the mind illumines the ancient teachings."

Mumon's commentary goes like this:

> The drama old Shakya puts on is a great hodgepodge. Just tell me now, Manjusri is the teacher of the seven buddhas—why couldn't he get the woman out of her samadhi when Momyo, a beginner, could? If you can firmly grasp this point, then for you this busy life of ignorance and discrimination will be the life of the dragon samadhi.

Buddhas and teachers say that fundamental wisdom, or prajna, is our birthright. And this fundamental wisdom is represented by, or symbolized by, Manjusri, the bodhisattva of wisdom—absolute wisdom. No one is without this wisdom. Even if one is blind or deaf or mute, one is whole and complete. Helen Keller is whole and complete. Shibayama-roshi says:

> This wisdom is the one truth to which everything returns and from which everything is born. If there is no dust in the eye, there

should be nothing in the universe to interfere with the sight. Is
there a distinction between satori and ignorance? Male and female? Entering into meditation and coming out of meditation?
There, just as it is, Manjusri's real worth is vividly revealed.
Don't be deluded by words. The live Manjusri pervades the universe. How wonderful it is that he could not bring the woman out
of her meditation.[1]

And then there is Momyo, the bodhisattva of the wisdom of differentiation. Shibayama-roshi says, " 'Differentiation' one may call it,
but where the differentiation wisdom shines, each and every thing,
as it is, is the entrance to emancipation."[2] Our minds are so used to
asking and dwelling on questions like, Why can one awaken her and
the other not? When the great conflagration at the end of the eon
comes, will my True Nature be destroyed or won't it? Has a dog buddha-nature, or hasn't it? Always the mind is oscillating from one
point to another, always it hovers on the surface of things like a bug
skating over the water. When you get down to the core, all such
questions vanish. We must see beyond the names. What does Manjusri mean, and what is Momyo? The teacher of the seven buddhas,
men, women, good, bad, they are nothing but "it." Our everyday life
as we know it is a mixture of good and bad, right and wrong, false
and true, gain and loss, life and death. Yet Mumon says that this ordinary life, our ordinary life just as it is, is a life of supreme awakening.
Our ordinary life? My ordinary life? What does he *mean*?
I hope you don't think he means that right and wrong, life and
death, cease to exist. When right or wrong no longer disturb one,
one transcends right and wrong. When at the deepest level life and
death—that is, constant change—no longer disturb, one is free from
life and death. If equality is stuck in equality, it ceases to be true
equality. "All is One" is not "it." What about all the differences?
Trees, spiders, clouds, good and bad. Will you ignore them to cling
to Oneness? Conversely, if differentiation is stuck at differentiation,
it is no longer true differentiation. Equality is the basis of differentiation. Differentiation is the dynamic working of equality. Facing the

world of differentiation, of struggle, from the ground of an insight into the world of equality, the world of emptiness—that is, the world of no-thingness—one is not caught up in designations. One is not limited by can or cannot, should or should not, may or may not, have or have not. Instead there's a tremendous, wonderful freedom. Emptiness isn't a negative void but is vastly alive and unbounded.

Of course people bring up the question, What do you do about right and wrong, about the lack of equality and all the terrible suffering in the world? Well, you do what you need to do, and you do what you can. The people who are the most effective have the insight and the calmness of mind to see into the truth of each situation and deal with it in a compassionate, courageous, and non-self-centered way. With a strong sense of "me and mine," however, there is often a great deal of uncertainty and fear. Self-centeredness breeds anxiety over winning and losing, gain and loss—which only makes it all the harder to be of real help. During the sixties and seventies many people tried to help get us out of the war in Vietnam and also establish a greater measure of equality in our society. Later many of them admitted, after they had gotten into one spiritual tradition or another, that the biggest reason for their failure was their own lack of centeredness, their own deep habit of seeing the world in terms of "us and them." Their own long addiction to self-centeredness was at the core of the problem, and because of this habitual limitation, they were unable to understand what they were really trying to do. To recognize the truth of one's limitations is the beginning of freedom. It is an endless practice.

Yet Mumon is even more exacting. He says that this busy life of ignorance and discrimination, *just as it is*, is the dragon samadhi, that is, it is itself the life of supreme satori.

Now we come to the verse:

One could awaken her, the other could not;
Both have their own freedom.
A god mask and a devil mask;
The failure is wonderful indeed.

One could awaken her and one could not. Mumon purposefully puts these opposing statements before us to demonstrate that we have to get beyond all such thinking. We may ask, in this connection, who could help an alcoholic better—a psychiatrist or an alcoholic in recovery? Many people might say a recovering alcoholic would be most effective. But that doesn't mean a psychiatrist couldn't help such a person either. Each has his or her own virtue. The same thing holds for Momyo and Manjusri. Momyo, the beginner, brings his wisdom and help. If we're beginners too, he might speak our language and help us a lot. But Manjusri, the great bodhisattva, certainly has his sphere of expertise. Each has his own freedom, a god mask and a devil mask. In our daily lives we assume all kinds of roles. At times, many times, we may slip on the mask of a devil and do terrible, thoughtless things both to ourselves and to others. Then, in our better moments, we may rise to godlike heights, demonstrating extreme altruism, compassion, and love. Everyone has his or her own capacities. We can't fault a person for not having the exact abilities that we may have. The same holds true with animals. People will say, "I love dogs, but I just can't stand cats." Ridiculous! A dog is a dog. A cat is a cat. Manjusri has his unique abilities and Momyo his. Maybe the highly knowledgeable pilot of a modern jet plane, with all its intricate complexities, would admire the deeply unified spiritual wisdom of Manjusri. Manjusri, in turn, might admire the jet pilot who could fly such an astonishingly complex machine. To be whole we need both kinds of wisdom.

What makes this such a wonderful world is its diversity. What if everybody were alike? What if everybody had the same abilities, the same talents and shortcomings? What a terrible, dreary, colorless world it would be. Mumon says, "The failure is wonderful indeed." Absolutely wonderful! A snake has no legs. Is it a failure compared to a bug, which has many? Each is just as it is. From the standpoint of awakening, there's no way to despise anyone or anything. Zen Master Rinzai said, "There's nothing in this world I dislike." Everything is what it is by reason of its karma. As karma changes, things change. Practicing diligently, our karma does change.

Often toward the end of a sesshin, even when one has been practicing diligently, there is a tendency to ease up, to feel, Well, I did
my best; I might as well take it easy now. This is to ignore a crucial
truth: all six previous days of honing the mind in zazen are now com-
pressed into the hours that remain. It would take another six whole
days of sitting to reach this point again. Because of this, there is a
vast amount of energy available to each one of us. It is not the time to
slacken our efforts but the time to make a devoted effort. We can do
better than we think we can, because we are more than we think we
are. Proust writes, "We are giants dipped in time." Zen Master
Eisai, one of Dogen's teachers, says in his *Propagation of Zen for the
Protection of the Country*:

> Great is Mind. Heaven's height is immeasurable, but Mind goes
> beyond heaven; the earth's depth is also unfathomable, but Mind
> reaches below the earth. The light of the sun and moon cannot be
> outdistanced, yet Mind passes beyond the light of sun and moon.
> The macrocosm is limitless, yet Mind travels outside the macro-
> cosm. How great is Space! How great the Primal Energy! Still
> Mind encompasses Space and generates the Primal Energy. Be-
> cause of it heaven covers and earth upbears. Because of it the sun
> and moon move on, the four seasons come in succession, and all
> things are generated. Great indeed is Mind![3]

In other words, all the energies of the universe come to consciousness
in each one of us.

These vast energies are prevented from functioning freely by our
ingrained fears and hopes, our conditioned and habitual thinking and
feeling, and so we fail to see "it," fail to realize "it." It's as if we
were to hold up our hand before our face and say, I've blocked out
the sun. We may momentarily be in shadow, but the sun nonetheless
is still shining as brightly as ever.

Sometimes practitioners ask, Well, what if I do have a slight
awakening? Is that really going to do a whole lot of good for myself
and others? In a famous line in the *Tao-te Ching*, Lao-tzu says, "A jour-

ney of a thousand miles begins with the first step." By practicing, by being in sesshin, one is taking a vital first step. A first awakening is another step. Each koan is a step forward on the endless road of practice. No matter how far we think we have gone, we can always go further. Every moment offers a fresh opportunity. Work diligently.

3

A Non-Buddhist

Questions the Buddha

THE GATELESS BARRIER, CASE 32

A non-Buddhist once asked the World-Honored One, "I do not ask for words, I do not ask for no words." The World-Honored One sat still. The non-Buddhist said admiringly, "The compassion of the World-Honored One has dispelled the clouds of my illusion and has enabled me to enter the Way." Making a deep bow of gratitude, he departed. Ananda, who was nearby, said to the Buddha, "What was it that this non-Buddhist realized that he so praised you?" The World-Honored One said, "A high-class horse moves at even the shadow of the whip."

COMMENTARY

Ananda was the Buddha's disciple, but his understanding was nothing like that of the non-Buddhist. How different are they, the Buddha's disciple and the non-Buddhist?

VERSE

Walking along the edge of a sword,
Running over jagged ice;
You need take no steps—
Let go your hold on the cliff!

The characters in this koan are Shakyamuni Buddha and his disciple, the venerable Ananda, who served the Buddha for over twenty-five years as his attendant. Ananda was also the Buddha's cousin and was known as the disciple with the best hearing and memory. There is also an unnamed non-Buddhist, probably a brahmin philosopher.

At the time of the Buddha, the Vedic tradition flourished widely in India. There were other profound teachings as well, such as the Jain. In fact, there were said to be ninety-six different philosophical schools in India at that time. Most of these leaned either toward materialism, emphasizing phenomena and the perceptions of the senses, or toward an extreme idealism that denied phenomenal differences, seeing them all as illusion. Mahayana Buddhism, on the other hand, upholds the teaching of the Middle Way. That is, it transcends both negative and affirmative views, subjectivism and objectivism, and is based on Reality itself, which is neither dualistic nor monistic.

One day a brahmin philosopher came to see the Buddha and asked to be shown directly the truth that is committed neither to an affirmative view with words, nor to a negative one without words. He may have already gone to see many teachers and was dissatisfied with the many answers he had received, none of which had opened his mind to Truth. Obviously he was a sincere aspirant. Notice the way his question was framed. If one speaks, one has already departed from the essential principle, for whatever one says is already limited and cannot be the whole truth. If one does not speak, one is not in accord with the phenomenal facts. So he is asking for the truth that transcends this dilemma. It is not a simple question. It's the kind of question that would come from a real philosopher. It is subtle, profound, and endowed with a real existential yearning.

"The World-Honored One sat still." Really look at an original Buddha figure sometime and you will get some idea of just how profoundly the Buddha sat when he "sat still." It was a dynamic sitting, with no sense of either "outer" or "inner," a condition of Absolute Oneness. If one had to describe it, one might say it was like an iron wall, or an impregnable fortress. In koan number eighty-four in the *Blue Cliff Record*, "Vimalakirti's Gate of Nonduality" (see chapter 4), in response to a question by Manjusri, the bodhisattva of wisdom, the great layman Vimalakirti also just sat. That is, he SAT! This sitting is often described in Zen as "the thundering silence of Vimalakirti." Such sitting is not mere silence or quietism. There are many kinds of silence. You could be silent when you don't know what to say. You could be silent purposely, to make a point. You could be silent in order to confuse an opponent in a debate. And then there is the profound silence which is expressed in poetic terms as "the silence ere the first word was spoke"—in other words, the silence which is the womb of all speech.

When one sits in this silent, deeply centered, selfless, unshakable way, it is called in Zen "acquiring a seat." Usually it's said that in a monastery, it takes a minimum of three years of daily zazen to acquire such a seat. And remember, in a monastery, people would be sitting a lot and attending sesshin regularly. What it also means is the ability to actively "sit" on every situation—to be present, centered, and steady regardless of circumstances. Ultimately such "sitting" must be understood in the widest sense. It is not just sitting with one's legs folded in the quiet of the zendo, but it is standing up, moving about, laughing, crying, eating, working. It is water flowing and clouds drifting. All are expressions of Absolute Reality. All are expressions of the Truth of our own nature. When we enter into every event of our lives singlemindedly—or, perhaps more accurately, no-mindedly—the true nature of Absolute Reality is being expressed. This is the fact that transcends the phenomenal world of restrictions and oppositions. The masters have expressed this in many seemingly different ways. Master Gu-tei raised a finger. Another raised a stick. Lin-chi (Rinzai) was famous for his shout. These are all perfect expressions of our True Nature, which is beyond all dualisms. In dynamic sitting, Shakyamuni is presenting everything. At the same time, we could say that he is presenting absolutely nothing at all.

In working on this koan, we also have to grasp what kind of a person the non-Buddhist was. If he were sitting in the presence of the Buddha to receive a blessing, the events of the koan would reflect a kind of *darshan*, as it is called in the Hindu tradition, in which a teacher silently gives spiritual blessing to a disciple or guest. But the non-Buddhist is not asking to receive a blessing, and the Buddha is not offering one.

Years ago when I was in India, I went to see a well-known teacher who was giving darshan. There were about a half-dozen of us seated on the floor around the teacher, who was sitting in a chair. Later I also went to darshan with a woman teacher who was well known in India, and that was quite a different scene. There were so many people and flowers! Garlands of flowers surrounded her, almost up to her waist. She was dressed in beautiful finery. We passed before her and made an offering of fruit, and I looked up at her as I bowed. Not everyone did that, but I did, and I saw a faint, archaic smile playing around her lips. There are many kinds of darshan, and Indian teachers still offer it today.

But those who write commentaries on this koan and say that the Buddha's presence—the nobility of his figure, or his power, his samadhi, his spiritual vibrations—got into the non-Buddhist and opened his mind in a darshan-like way, are off the mark. Which doesn't mean that the Buddha's vivid, radiant presence did not inspire the non-Buddhist to make a leap. This can happen. But as the Buddha himself, according to tradition, said just prior to his parinirvana, "A man must take medicine to be cured; the mere sight of the physician is not enough. Likewise, the mere sight of Me enables no one to conquer suffering; he will have to meditate for himself on the gnosis I have communicated."[1] We see from this that the Buddha emphasized one's own actual practice, training, and insight.

Getting back to the non-Buddhist, he must have been desperate, wholeheartedly yearning for truth, and thus ripe for an inner transformation. When you stop to think of it, to go before a teacher, especially one as renowned as the Buddha, and say, "I do not ask for words, I do not ask for no words," is a very bold thing to do. Usually when you go before someone who is very well known and well regarded, you don't ask for anything at all. Instead you gratefully take what is offered. Imagine going before the Dalai Lama, let's say, and instead of just bowing gratefully, you make some sort of spiritual demand or present a challenge!

Perhaps the non-Buddhist was well known himself, maybe even something of a teacher. Whoever he was, he was desperate—in the best sense of the word. He was as desperate as a person whose head is underwater. Air! Air! is all that person is thinking. It might not even be conscious. One's whole being is just, Air! Having gone to so many philosophers and teachers and finding no relief for his anguish, the non-Buddhist was like a drowning person. He was at an extremity, deep in spiritual searching. Suddenly he saw that the truth was beyond all words and beyond all no-words, and he came to awakening.

One Japanese Zen master, Engo, commenting on this, asks, "Tell me, what is the great compassion of the World-Honored One?" It's a very good question, really. What is the great compassion of a great teacher? What is the compassion of the dharma ancestors? Master Shibayama adds, "I want an answer not concerned with words or no-words."[2]

Then the non-Buddhist says that the Buddha "has enabled me to enter the Way." This truth that transcends affirmation and negation can be neither attained nor lost. It is the birthright of each one of us, and the non-Buddhist was simply awakened to what he had always had from the very beginning. We all have "it" from the very beginning. At that moment of awakening, the World-Honored One and the non-Buddhist were "not-two." There was no World-Honored One, and there was no non-Buddhist. The Buddha just sat, and the naked truth was right there. One doesn't have to be a Buddhist to have "it" or to get "it." In fact, one can't be anything at all to get "it"! Zen Master Hakuin, in his famous *Song in Praise of Zazen*, says, "From the very beginning, all beings are Buddha."[3]

Then we come to the second half of the koan. We can imagine that Ananda, the Buddha's attendant and close disciple—a true Buddhist, yet one who had not yet had an awakening—was deeply puzzled, even chagrined, maybe even envious when he heard the non-Buddhist say, "The compassion of the World-Honored One . . . has enabled me to enter the Way." And so there was a real need to understand when he says to the Buddha, "What was it that this non-Buddhist realized that he so praised you?"

The World-Honored One replied, "A high-class horse moves at even the shadow of the whip." One of the sutras, the *Samyuktagama*, describes the different qualities of Buddhist practitioners. In it the Buddha says that practitioners can be compared to four different kinds of horses. The first senses the shadow of the whip and instantly obeys the rider's will. The second reacts a bit later, when its hair is touched by the whip. The third does not start until its flesh is cut. The fourth moves only when its bones are forcefully shaken. This is further clarified. The first class, those who move to the will of the rider at even the shadow of the whip, are like those people who feel the impermanence of the world when they hear of the death of someone far off, not in their own village, that is, not personally known to them. The second kind, those who are like the horse who moves when its hair is touched, feel the impermanence of the world only when they hear of the death of someone they personally know. The third horse, which starts when its hide is cut, are those people who feel the impermanence of the world only when they are faced with death in their own family. And the fourth kind, those who start when the whip reaches the bone, are like those people who don't feel the impermanence of the world until personally faced with their own serious illness or death.

In other words, these similes indicate the depth of a person's causal relation to the felt need for practice. It begins with the first noble truth of suffering, an awareness of universal impermanence and the sense of loss and anxiety—dread, even—that this awareness awakens in us. The first noble truth is of our own pain, which is the world's pain. The second reveals the fundamental cause of that anguish. The third is that there is a path beyond such suffering. The way of practice, and not just philosophy, begins here.

Now we might well inquire, where does Ananda fit in all this? He was the Buddha's own cousin, noble, clear-minded, spiritually sensitive, and highly intelligent. He had spent many years with the Buddha. He had talked with him, walked with him, sat with him in daily zazen and in many long retreats, and had heard nearly all his dharma talks, or teishos. So why didn't he know what the non-Buddhist, someone who had never spent time with the Buddha before, now knew?

Responding to Ananda, the Buddha says, "A high-class horse moves at even the shadow of the whip." Zen Master Shibayama quotes another Zen master who comments on the Buddha's answer to Ananda: "You are too mild and easy, World-Honored One. Had I been there I would have slapped Ananda without a word. Then Ananda might have been revived with even greater vigor than the non-Buddhist." Shibayama observes: "For a Zen master this is but a natural comment."[4]

We see here also the qualities of the different Buddhist countries. The style of Indian Buddhism is different than the style of Zen, born as it is out of China. But it is also true that Zen masters everywhere, even in Japan, have different personalities and different styles. Not everyone uses slaps and cracks and shouts, and this was certainly true in ancient China as well. Rinzai (Lin-chi) was known for his dramatic shout. Yet of Joshu (Chao-chou) it was said, "His lips flash light." That is, his manner was very quiet and mild, yet absolutely incisive and profound. In his quiet way perhaps he could accomplish more than Rinzai, with his shaking and slapping and shouting. It is almost impossible to make any kind of dogmatic statements about these kinds of things. There are all sorts of teachers, and, depending on their own training, their own degree of awakening, but mostly on their own temperament, they will use different methods. The important thing is to realize that without hard and sincere training and discipline, it's virtually impossible to attain a deep awakening or to further deepen an initial one.

Is Ananda being scolded by the Buddha? Is there some implied criticism buried in the response about the high-class horse? Is the Buddha saying to Ananda, The non-Buddhist took right off and ran the whole race, but you have hardly left the gate?

Now we come to the commentary. "Ananda was the Buddha's disciple, but his understanding was nothing like that of the non-Buddhist. How different are they, the Buddha's disciple and the non-Buddhist?" The question remains, why couldn't Ananda come to awakening? He was with the Buddha for twenty-five years. Here is the non-Buddhist, a man who is a philosopher and therefore, like Ananda, of a decidedly intellectual bent. Yet he came to awakening with just this brief contact with the Buddha, while Ananda, who was constantly with the Buddha, could not.

Sometimes it's said in Buddhism, in describing the teacher-student relationship, that if you get too close to the teacher you are in danger of being burned, but if you're too far away, you are in danger of being frozen. The Middle Way is to be close to the teacher, but not too close. And we can imagine that because Ananda was constantly with his teacher—the Buddha, his own cousin—in a sense he was too close to absorb the Buddha's real, existential teaching. He loved and respected the man, but he didn't see the teaching, didn't get how it really related to himself. He was so busy, too, making sure that all the Buddha's talks had been committed to memory that he never really took in the deep, life-changing import of those precious words. In fact, it wasn't until the Buddha had entered parinirvana that Ananda became really ripe for teaching. And under Mahakashyapa, who then took over guidance of the order, he attained enlightenment. Yet Ananda was really quite a remarkable man. He was very admired and loved by the women because he was always defending them and speaking up for them with the Buddha. The nuns would go to him when they had difficult problems relating to practice. He was sensitive, kind, intelligent, compassionate, trustworthy.

In an absolute sense, it doesn't matter at all whether you're a Buddhist or a non-Buddhist. Non-Buddhists as well as Buddhists have the buddha-nature; they are, as are all beings, buddhas. As the Buddha is said to have spontaneously proclaimed at the moment of his great enlightenment, wonder of wonders, all beings are intrinsically, from the very first, buddhas! All already possess, from the very beginningless beginning, the true Essential Nature. So all can, whether Buddhist or not, awaken to "It."

What is the point, then, of allying oneself with Buddhism and the Buddhist tradition? Why become—if one can be said to "become" anything—a Buddhist? To be blunt, what is the advantage? It is simple: Buddhist tradition and teaching embody profound and intimate knowledge of the human mind. Many kinds of teachings, many kinds of devotions are part of Buddhism, as, of course, they are of most religions. Buddhism, too, has an elaborate philosophy and an elaborate psychology. Through the centuries, masters and teachers have developed many ways to help us hone, refine, and eventually awaken the mind to its own True Nature. That is the aim, we might say, of Buddhism—not to have us simply become believers, but to have us each become a buddha, to have us awaken and live lives of deepening compassion and wisdom. Koans themselves, which are the uniquely creative legacy of Chinese Zen, are one prime example of the kind of help and guidance the tradition offers. In short, the tradition helps make our own awakening possible. Does one need to be a Buddhist to awaken? No. But it can truly help.

Most of us practicing today began our spiritual lives as non-Buddhists. The non-Buddhist who comes with genuine life questions, who feels the impermanence of life and yet who senses there is something beneath all the flux and anguish, awakens. As the koan shows, this has always been so. We each lack nothing. Buddhist tradition reminds us of this and helps us stay focused on the goalless Goal. Once we make a commitment to the living tradition, all this works naturally for us. There's no strain, no Should I? Shouldn't I?

Recently I received a letter from a thoughtful person who is writing a book. He wanted to know if I could contribute some thoughts

to his view that Americans are bent on amassing material things because they feel a deep emptiness in their lives. In my response I talked
about commitment. Commitment doesn't mean a formal commitment,
necessarily, but committing oneself to any activity or enterprise is
really the first step toward developing the qualities that are necessary
for success in that venture, whatever it happens to be. The simplest
things require it. *Wholeheartedness* might be an alternate term.

We each have our own ways, our own strengths and weaknesses.
Different things may draw different people to practice. Even the
same person will be motivated at different times in different ways.
Ananda persisted in his practice and eventually became a dharma ancestor himself.

Mumon's verse is:

Walking along the edge of a sword,
Running over jagged ice;
You need take no steps—
Let go your hold on the cliff!

Spiritual training has been called walking a razor's edge, and rightly
so. It is demanding, and great care and concentration are required.
Walking along the edge of a sword also suggests going through great
danger at the risk of one's life. That metaphor is appropriate. In Zen
practice we must focus and concentrate as if our very life depended
on it—our real life does. In doing zazen, one may drip with sweat
even in an unheated room. The focus of the mind is that intense. It is
like running along the edge of a sword. One slip and . . . Mumon is
really praising the non-Buddhist. And he is also pointing out a path
of practice for each of us.

In Zen it's said, "One leap into enlightenment." The great philosopher Kierkegaard also talks of making an existential leap, of not following a logical progression but of taking a leap beyond logic and
reason into intuition itself. On this level there is no distinction between non-Buddhist and Buddhist or any other such distinctions.
Man, woman, wise person, ignorant person—none of these distinc-

tions are relevant. Mumon is saying this too when he says, "You need take no steps—Let go your hold on the cliff!" There's nothing you need to do, no knowledge you need to gain, no wisdom you need to attain. Just let go, and you're already there. Wonder of wonders! From the beginning all beings are Buddha!

What does a cliff suggest? That where you are now is risky. At any time you could fall and be dashed on the rocks below. A cliff symbolizes the circumstances of our everyday life to which we desperately cling. We grasp at one idea after another, one self-image after another, one job after another, one person after the next. We cling to ideas of being a Buddhist or non-Buddhist. Let go of all such delusions, Mumon advises, drop all fixed notions of this or that, all ideas of how things should be or should not be. There's no need to bind oneself at all. Just fully let go, and all things are as they are. Of course, this doesn't mean one ignores responsibilities or ethics.

Zen Master Hakuin has a verse that goes something like this: "Hey, youngster, if you don't want to die, die now. Once dead, you won't have to die twice." An ancient Christian monk, a non-Buddhist, said, "He who dies before he dies, does not die when he dies." A Zen master also said, "Having died one death, here is a person free and serene." To live, one must die. One must let go completely, dying to all that one has accumulated, all that one has grasped. Buddhist, non-Buddhist, let it all go! Then you, too, will realize.

Realize what?

What did the non-Buddhist realize? It's not just Ananda's question, but a question for each of us.

PART TWO

Koans

of the

Great

Lay

Practitioners

4

Vimalakirti's Gate
of Nonduality

BLUE CLIFF RECORD, CASE 84

Vimalakirti asked Manjusri, "What is the bodhisattva's dharma gate of nonduality?"

Manjusri answered, "To my mind, in all dharmas there are no words, no preaching, no demonstration, and no recognition. It is beyond all questions and answers. That is entering the dharma gate of nonduality."

Then Manjusri asked Vimalakirti, "Each of us has spoken. Now tell us, good man, what is the bodhisattva's entry into the dharma gate of nonduality?"

COMMENTARY

Setcho comments, saying, "What will Vimalakirti say?" And again he says, "I have seen through him." In another translation this is presented as, "I understand."

Yuima, as he is known to the Japanese, or Vimalakirti, his original Sanskrit name (which means "spotless purity"), was a very wealthy, successful, and spiritually developed householder of the Buddha's time who resided in the city of Vaisali. Did he really exist? He has existed through the ages. He is greater than facts and dates. The *Vimalakirti Sutra*, which reveals his sayings and doings, has been one of the most highly regarded and popular of all Buddhist texts, especially in China. (There are several good English translations. Richard Robinson, who taught Buddhism at the University of Wisconsin, did a fine translation that has never been published. Most of my quotes in this talk are from a manuscript of his text, with some editing and modifications. There is now also a good translation by Robert Thurman from Tibetan, and one by Burton Watson from Chinese. The sutra can be a wonderful inspiration for laypeople, presenting as it does the words and deeds of a great lay figure.)

Engo, the Chinese Zen master who wrote the introductory words and also the afterword to the cases of the *Blue Cliff Record*, writes this introduction to the koan:

> To say "Yes" does not necessarily make it yes. To say "No" does not necessarily make it no. Get away from yes and no. Forget receiving and losing and become utterly naked. Now what is this in front of me and what is this behind me? Some monk may come before you and say, "In front of you is the main hall and the temple gate and behind you is the sleeping room and the guest room." Would you say that one kept open eyes? If any of you think that you can discern the thoughts of such persons, it would be well for you to examine carefully the characters and doings of the ancients.

This koan deals with the subject of nonduality. "To say 'Yes' does not necessarily make it yes. To say 'No' does not necessarily make it no." What does this mean? We constantly find people strongly saying yes to some things and no to others. Others may have similarly strong responses, but in the opposite way. Often, all too often, fights break out between individuals and even between nations out of this yes and no, out of this strong sense of duality.

Our lives and relationships are so often filled with phrases and thoughts like, I'm right, you're wrong. Yes, I'm right. No, you're wrong. But Engo is saying that to truly live we must transcend yes and no. We must express the totality of which yes and no are only one small piece. Because a yes-and-no perspective is limited, it is ultimately untrue. Every yes stands against a no. It is conditioned by no, and, conversely, every no is conditioned by yes. They are mutually conditioned. There is a Christian expression known as "the eternal yea." What kind of yes is that? It is a Zen *Yes!* Not the yes of yes-and-no, but the *Yes!* of the spirit that affirms our total being. That *Yes!* is the sound of the whole universe. It stands against nothing. Nothing stands against it.

In a Zen monastery you are taught that when someone asks you to do something, immediately you just say, *"Hai!"* Yes! No premeditation. No weighing and analyzing. No thinking, Should I do it, should I not do it? But at once just *Yes!* Of course, in a monastery you're not going to be asked to do something reprehensible, something that violates the precepts. In another situation you might, indeed, need to think carefully about what you've been asked to do. You could make terrible mistakes. German officers after World War II said they were just following orders: Put these people on cattle cars. *Jawohl!* Yes! In ordinary circumstances, not only is it wise to leave room for thought and consideration, but often it is crucial.

Still, taking it to extremes, some people become so habituated to weighing and analyzing that they become tight and closed up, like a flower shut in on itself for the night. They remain locked within a self-created cocoon of their own limited thoughts, without flow or openness or genuine affirmation. The spring breezes cease to blow for them. The wide earth becomes cramped and narrow. The *Yes!* aspect of Zen training can free frozen energies. Saying *Yes!* with a capital Y—responding wholeheartedly to every situation—affirms one's True Nature and can be deeply transformative. It is Self-affirmation. It is not just a technique. You can just as easily say *Yes!* to thinking something through as anything else. It doesn't at all have to mean ignoring thought.

Engo lays a dilemma before us: "What is this in front of me and what is this behind me? Some monk may come before you and say, 'In front of you is the main hall and the temple gate and behind you is the sleeping room and the guest room.' Would you say that one kept open eyes?"

If Engo asked you whether the monk's eyes were open, what would you say? If the temple hall and the temple gate were in front of you and you were asked what was in front of you, you wouldn't say the sleeping room and the guest room, would you? And if you were asked what was behind you, you wouldn't say the main hall and the temple gate. But what would you say? If you say the main hall, the temple gate, the sleeping room, the guest room, it all falls into the realm of discrimination. It's a discrimination of the part from the whole. The world is chopped up into little pieces. What's there? Oh, this piece and that piece.

In the end, it all depends on what your answer arises from, what it demonstrates. What is in front? Main hall. What is in back? The sleeping room. What is in back? The guest room. Or what is in back—the sleeping room? Yes! Is the guest room in back? Yes!

One time a monk and I were taking a walk, and we saw a bird. Pointing to it, I asked the monk, "Without discriminating, what would you call it?" "It's a bird!" he answered. A bird is a bird is a bird! And, if it's a bird, then it's really more than a bird. But can you say what that more is? No. You can only truly say, It's a bird. Don't try to say that which is more than a bird. Why not? *It's a bird!* A rose is a rose is a rose. What is it? A rose!

This koan of the encounter between Vimalakirti and Manjusri has been lifted almost directly out of the great Mahayana Buddhist text *The Vimalakirti Sutra*. Not only was this sutra highly regarded for its profundity, but it was enormously popular with monks and lay practitioners alike. Perhaps this is because it is not only immensely profound but iconoclastic, dramatic, and humorous. It remains one of the most highly revered sutras in Zen.

Sutras are usually the purported teachings, or dharma talks, of the Buddha himself, as remembered by his cousin and attendant, Ananda, said to have had perfect aural memory. What he heard he remembered, exactly as it was originally spoken. Thus every sutra begins with the traditional formula, "Thus have I heard." This is the voice of our dharma ancestor Ananda. But the *Vimalakirti Sutra* is unique. Rather than being about the Buddha or a compilation of the words and teachings of the Buddha, it is about a householder. In fact, it is one of the only two texts accorded the status of sutra that are not records of the Buddha's own words. The other such unique sutra is the *Platform Sutra of the Sixth Patriarch,* which presents the life, words, and deeds of Hui-neng, the Sixth Patriarch of Zen in China. Interestingly, he was also a layperson until very far on in his religious career.

Vimalakirti, his sutra tells us, had worshiped countless buddhas in past lives. He made offerings, followed their teachings, and thereby established deep roots of goodness. After eons he attained to the utmost wisdom and skillfulness, acquiring the limitless patience of the Unborn, or Unconditioned Mind. His insight and eloquence were completely unimpeded. He was able to fearlessly "sport" in the superknowledges and completely triumph over Mara, the Buddhist tempter or devil, who entices us, time and time again, toward selfishness, anger, and anxiety.

The Buddha's own final confrontation with Mara is one of the high points of all the great legendary accounts of his enlightenment. In that dramatic, mythic moment, the Future Buddha calls on the earth to witness for him. Actually, Mara first sends his beautiful daughters to tempt the Buddha with desire. But they do not succeed. Then he sends an army of horrific demons to terrify him. They, also, cannot move him. Then, in some versions, Mara himself at last comes before the Future Buddha seeking to find some tiny chink in the Buddha's armor of total commitment and concentration. He too fails.

We each have our Maras. We each are tested. Vimalakirti had triumphed over them all. His great vows—the four great bodhisattva vows which all Zen students repeat daily at the close of formal sessions of zazen—were fulfilled. These vows are:

All beings without number I vow to liberate.
Endless blind passions I vow to uproot.

Dharma gates beyond measure I vow to penetrate.
The great way of Buddha I vow to attain.

Vimalakirti's mind, the sutra tells us, was as vast as the ocean.
The title *Dalai Lama* means something very similar, a teacher whose
mind is as vast as the ocean. So this way of looking at the mind and
of honoring one who has attained such understanding is very old in
Buddhism and is probably part of all Buddhist traditions.

All the buddhas commended Vimalakirti. Shakyamuni Buddha is
the buddha of our world and our historical time. There are countless
buddhas—fully realized, fully awakened beings—throughout the
endless universe. According to Buddhist teaching, there have been
buddhas on this earth before Shakyamuni and there will be buddhas
after. The next buddha-to-be, Maitreya, is currently in the Tushita
Heavens preparing the compassionate and skillful means to save all
deluded and suffering beings. Millions of years from now it will be
his turn to put a shoulder to the dharma wheel on this earth and give
it a good turn.

Vimalakirti, the sutra tells us, was revered by disciples and respected by the lords of the world—which means not just kings but
gods, that is, beings of the deva realm. There are six unenlightened
realms in the mythic universe of classical Buddhist tradition: the
realms of human beings and of animals—which are visible to normal
sight—and the realms of the gods, of the warring titans, of the hungry ghosts, and of the hell-dwellers. Sometimes these are viewed as
actual geographic realms. Sometimes they are interpreted as psychological states. Watching the glamorous lives of movie stars and the
super-rich may give us an inkling of the realm of the devas. Interestingly, it is said in the sutras that when a deva is about to fall from its
heavenly condition, its garlands of flowers wither and it begins to
smell bad. It becomes terrified, devastated to lose its karmically conditioned state of attraction, splendor, and lofty—but still partial—
freedom. It is devastated because it now remembers that even this
exalted condition is only temporary, karmically conditioned, and so
is not ultimate liberation at all. When a deva falls from such a heav-

enly state, it falls hard, and its sense of loss is overwhelmingly painful. Watching the news, we may all too often also see hell. War, famine, destruction, violence, and disaster abound. The condition of hell is mythic but no myth. Its sufferings are very real, after all.

Because Vimalakirti wished only to help deluded and suffering beings, he practiced skillful means in his own city of Vaisali. The sutra says something about that skillfulness too. It tells us that his wealth was boundless—and so he attracted the poor. Keeping the precepts in spotless purity, he attracted transgressors. His patience and noble conduct were faultless, and, through them, he attracted the hostile and angry. With his limitless energy and vigor he attracted those who were indolent and lazy.

Vimalakirti provides us with a wonderful model for an active and engaged lay life. He is wisdom itself and compassion itself and skillfulness itself—awake in, deeply involved in and with the realities of his time and place. He was truly "in the world but not of it."

The attraction of opposites is interesting. Certainly the wealthy do attract the poor. Those who are pure do seem to draw the impure to them. Those who are hostile and angry do seem to seek out those with patience and calmness. And those with great vigor draw to them the less energetic. Vimalakirti, having attained these inner riches, let them flourish for the sake of others. He had a magnetic personality and used it to help convert and guide others along the path of truth. Whoever came his way he helped. In the tenth and last scene of the ten ox-herding pictures, those famous ink paintings of 12th-century China that map the stages of Zen realization, part of the final verse accompanying the painting says, "Without recourse to mystic powers, withered trees he swiftly brings to bloom."[1] So it was with Vimalakirti—a fully conscious, fully realized personality. Those who met him discovered their own innate freedom, their own long-hidden compassion and wisdom.

Of course, it isn't always true that opposites attract. The lazy can also attract the lazy. Drunkards can attract other drunkards. But when the buddha-mind functions even a little bit, we do seem to be attracted to those qualities we lack. Actually the buddha-mind has no qualities; nothing can be said about it. Anything that could be said would be a limitation. Nonetheless, when it is operating freely, unimpeded insight and vigor and patience and purity are its nature and will manifest themselves.

The sutra says that Vimalakirti remained a layman. He never took monastic vows. Yet while he fully lived the householder's life, he was not attached to it; he was not attached to the three realms at all. The highest of the three realms is the realm of no-form; Below that lies the realm of form; and lower still is the realm of desire. Sometimes these three are referred to as the triple world, which can also mean the past, future, and present, for the universe extends horizontally as well as vertically. Vimalakirti was not attached to any realm whatsoever.

So the sutra says that while he ate and he drank, his taste was for the pleasures of meditation. He went happily to places of gambling and amusement, but only to save others. He engaged in business and gained profits, but he did not confine his pleasure to them, and he used his success to benefit the community. He roamed the crossroads to bring benefit to wanderers. He entered the courts to defend those who were defenseless. He entered the classrooms to help educate children. He entered the brothels to reveal the errors of lust. He entered taverns and established people's resolve. When he was with the rich he was regarded as the best among them and preached the highest dharma. When he was with householders he was considered the best among them, for he showed how to sever greed. When he was with the warriors, he was the best among them and taught patience. When he was with brahmins, those of the highest, purest class, he was the best among them and removed arrogance. When he was with the great ministers, he was the best among them and taught the just dharma. In his own time and place he was seen as a model of all that is good, trustworthy, and noble. For the sake of others he taught freely, in all the ordinary circumstances of life, by precept and by example, releasing his fellows from snares and difficulties.

One of the reasons why Vimalakirti is such a remarkable figure and has had such a pull on the Buddhist imagination these last twenty-five centuries is surely that while he was a fully spiritually developed person, he was totally successful and capable in a worldly sense as well. In him the split between worldliness and spirituality seems healed. In fact, it seems not to exist at all. We live in a culture in which mind and body, worldliness and spirituality remain at war. Wealth, which is sought after as if it were the greatest of goals, is also, at the same time, viewed suspiciously, seen as a likely source of ethical and spiritual ruin. In Vimalakirti we sense wholeness, potentially our own wholeness. There is nothing dualistic about him.

So Vimalakirti didn't find it necessary to give up his wealth in order to live a spiritual life—unlike another noted layman, the famous Layman P'ang of T'ang era China. Vimalakirti lived freely with his wealth. He used it wisely, not being tied to it. P'ang, on the other hand, seemed to have felt that wealth was bound to be a source of spiritual trouble. The records of his life say that he tossed his money in a lake or river so that it would be beyond his own reach and the reach of others. Perhaps this says something about the difference between myth and history, the ideal and the actual. Vimalakirti may have been a historical person. We don't know. But through the sutra, at least, he has become a mythic figure and reveals an archetype. He shows what is possible. P'ang, on the other hand, was a real historical personage.

It's interesting that the three most famous laymen in Buddhism—Fu Daishi and Layman P'ang in China and Vimalakirti in India—were such completely different types. What they had in common was a deeply enlightened view of existence, as well as great compassion and patience. Indeed, they each showed a full measure of all the noble qualities of developed human character.

The sutra says that through limitless skillful means, Vimalakirti allowed his body to show the appearance of illness. Because of this, numberless people—kings, ministers, wealthy householders, brahmins, princes, and high officials—all came to inquire about his welfare. And when they came, Vimalakirti took the opportunity to preach the dharma to them. He even used illness as a skillful means (*upaya* in Sanskrit) to advance beings on the Great Way—which is a literal meaning of *mahayana* in Mahayana Buddhism (*maha* in Sanskrit means great; *yana* is vehicle or way). As the Buddha reveals in the *Lotus Sutra*, the Great Way is the way or vehicle that already includes or carries all beings. It is the way all beings are already proceeding, the way of spiritual evolution and enlightenment.

Adapting the teachings to the needs of the listeners and skillfully using opportunities as they arise to reveal the Truth typifies the Buddhist approach. Vimalakirti uses his illness as a way of teaching those who have come to console him. He teaches impermanence, one of the three characteristics of existence. Revealing impermanence, he encourages his guests to aspire to perfect enlightenment and to attain the invulnerable body born of wisdom, compassion, and virtue.

Now the sutra tells us that the rich man, Vimalakirti, thought to himself, "Here I lie sick in bed. Why does the Blessed One, the Buddha, not have compassion for me?" The Buddha, the sutra also tells us, instantly knew this thought. And so begins the drama that will bring our protagonists, Manjusri and Vimalakirti, together. The Buddha says to Shariputra, one of his closest disciples, "Go call upon Vimalakirti and inquire about his sickness."[2]

But, surprisingly, Shariputra begs off, answering, in effect, "I don't think I'm ready to go, Blessed One. I was once meditating under a tree when Vimalakirti came to me and said, 'You don't need to sit still for long hours like this. That's not real silent sitting. Not to display body or mind in the three realms is true sitting. Not to relinquish religious qualities and yet to display the traits of the worldly, this is still sitting. With the mind neither abiding inside nor lying outside—this is still sitting. Not severing passions yet entering nirvana, this is still sitting. Whoever can sit in this way is sealed with the approval of the Buddha.' Honored One," says Shariputra, "I was dumbfounded and didn't know how to respond. That man's insight and eloquence are overwhelming. Please ask someone else to go."

In *The Three Pillars of Zen* there is a famous mondo in which a Chinese monk, who later became Baso, a great master (Ma-tsu in Chinese; his dates are 709–788), is doing zazen, and doing more zazen. His teacher, Nangaku (Nan-yueh, 677–744) comes and asks him why he is doing all this zazen. Baso answers, "To become a buddha." The master picks up a tile and starts to polish it. Baso asks, "What are you doing?" "I'm polishing this tile to make a mirror," answers Nangaku. "How can polishing turn a tile into a mirror?" "How can sitting turn you into a buddha?" This is not to say that sitting is not necessary. In all the history of Zen, only the Sixth Patriarch is said to have had genuine enlightenment without doing zazen. (In Zen circles it is said that he had done a lot of zazen in his past life.) No, it's the thought of "turning into" that is at issue.

The Chinese genius is at work here in our koan. The Indian extravagance and love of words for their own sake, as we see them in the sutra, are reduced to bare essentials, and the grip of paradox is added to make the teaching hit the mind and really stick. Still, Indian as he is, Vimalakirti is being very Zen-like. He strips Shariputra's mind of the notion that simply sitting and doing zazen will turn him into a buddha. He takes away all ideas of attaining something, all notions of dualistic practice, all attachments to the form.

Then the Buddha says to Maudgalyayana, another great disciple, "You go and call on Vimalakirti to inquire about his sickness." Probably the Buddha knew well where this was all heading. He was setting the drama in motion. Then Maudgalyayana essentially replies, "Blessed One, I can't go either." And he tells his own story of meeting Vimalakirti while out preaching. Once again Vimalakirti had taken everything to another level, just pulled the ground right out from under the feet of one of the Buddha's greatest disciples, ran verbal and spiritual circles around him, and left him tongue-tied and dumbfounded.

And so it goes with all the great disciples. Each has his own tale to tell that pretty much concludes, "And so you see, World-Honored One, I'm not spiritually developed enough to call on him and inquire about his sickness."

Then the Buddha turns to the great enlightened bodhisattvas. But amazingly, they too all admit that they have been bested in dharma encounter with the old layman, and not one of them feels up to going.

At last the Buddha turns to Manjusri, who is the bodhisattva of wisdom itself. "Now, you go and call on Vimalakirti and inquire about his sickness."

Manjusri answers the Buddha, saying, "O Blessed One, the man is hard to respond to. His eloquence is unchecked and his wisdom unobstructed. He knows the dharma. He has opened up all the buddha treasuries. He vanquishes the many Maras. He sports in the super-knowledges. His wisdom and his skillful means have all passed beyond. Nevertheless I will accept the Buddha's request and go call on him and ask about his sickness." What, after all, can Manjusri do? As the embodiment of wisdom, he has to go. So he girds his loins, as it were, and sets off.

Then all the thousands of bodhisattvas and disciples and *shakras* and *brahmas* and other kings of the gods gathered there think, "If these two greatly spiritually developed beings, Manjusri and Vimalakirti, meet, surely an exciting and enlightening dharma exchange will occur." Naturally all eight thousand bodhisattvas, five hundred disciples, and hundred thousand gods decide to go along. So Manjusri, attended by a huge crowd, at last enters the city of Vaisali. The moment of our drama has come.

Vimalakirti, with his vast powers of awareness, knows they are coming. By magic power he empties his room, removing everything except the bed on which he lies. When Manjusri enters, the room is empty. Only Vimalakirti is there, lying on his sickbed. Starting the dharma exchange at once, Vimalakirti says, "Manjusri, you come in the guise of not-coming. You see in the guise of not-seeing." Manjusri replies, "So it is, Householder. When I come there is no coming. When I go there is no going. For what reason? One who comes, comes from nowhere. One who goes, reaches nowhere. But let us put this matter aside for a while. Householder, from what source does your illness arise? How long is it since it arose? How will it cease?"

As they talk, all the many thousands who had followed slip into Vimalakirti's empty sickroom with Manjusri. All fit in. The room is so empty it is beyond limitation.

Vimalakirti's response is also without limits. He says, "My illness has arisen from ignorance and craving for existence. Because all living beings are sick, I am sick." His words still echo today, remaining among the most famous words in Buddhism. "I am sick because all beings are sick with the sicknesses of greed, anger, and delusion," he says. "When this sickness in all living beings ceases, then my sickness will cease." Vimalakirti sums up the mind and way of the bodhi-sattva in one sentence. If others suffer, we all suffer. Only when all are free from suffering can the bodhisattva be truly happy. We see here the indivisibility of all existence. What happens to one happens to everybody. None of us can say, I'm not my brother's keeper. If there's no happiness for others, then there's no happiness for us. It is Vimalakirti's fundamental teaching—"not-twoness."

This being India, not China, however, Vimalakirti goes on. He says that the bodhisattva is reborn for the sake of teaching living be-ings. This is part of the skillful means of the bodhisattva. And yet he says, "If there is rebirth there is sickness." As long as we have a body, as long as we crave for rebirth, for future existence, inevitably there will be sickness. If we had no body, what would there be to get sick? The body is the crystallization of our own thoughts. Then he says it's just like the parents of an only child. "When the child gets sick, the father and mother also get sick. When the child gets better, the father and mother also get better. The bodhisattva similarly loves all living beings. When living beings are sick, the bodhisattva is sick. When living beings recover, the bodhisattva is also better. You ask from what ground does this sickness arise? The bodhisattva's sickness arises from great compassion."

The bodhisattva's sickness arises from great compassion. And in Mahayana Buddhism, of which this text is a primary exemplar, the bodhisattva will not get well until all beings are also well—that is, until all have awakened to truth and are liberated from the sickness of delusion. I will not enter nirvana until all beings have entered nir-vana: this is the gist of the great compassionate vow of the bodhi-sattva. But it is also simply the truth. Well, this should give you the flavor of it. Vimalakirti is a very wise, very spiritually developed person.

Actually the dharma-jousting of this great pair, Manjusri and Vimalakirti, continues a bit further. In response to Vimalakirti's final long and profound discourse, the sutra tells us that eight thousand gods conceived the spirit of perfect unexcelled enlightenment! At this point nothing should surprise us, for in this sutra anything is possible.

Indeed, after that, several truly miraculous events occur. In one, thirty-two thousand gigantic and splendid lion thrones are manifested in Vimalakirti's tiny sickroom. In another, a goddess suddenly appears in the tiny room and, through a humorous and profound dialogue (and a magical transformation of Shariputra into a woman!), reveals that while there is, indeed, perfect enlightenment, there is no attainment of perfect enlightenment. Do you see why this must be so?

Now the stage is set, and we arrive at the events of our koan proper. Vimalakirti raises a challenge to all the assembled bodhisattvas, asking, "Good sirs, how does the bodhisattva enter the dharma realm of nonduality?"

Then, one after another, thirty-two bodhisattvas each give an explanation of how they themselves, in their own practice, entered the dharma gate of nonduality. One says, "Arising and ceasing are two. The dharma originally did not arise, so it has no cessation. Getting this is entering the dharma realm of nonduality." Another says, " 'I' and 'mine' are two. Because there is 'I' there is 'mine.' If there is no 'I,' there is no 'mine.' This is entering the realm of nonduality."

The final bodhisattva, named Satyarata, or Delight in Truth, says, "Truth and untruth are dualistic. But when one sees truly, one does not even see truth, so how can there be untruth?"

When all the bodhisattvas have recounted a personal experience of nonduality they ask Manjusri, "How does the bodhisattva enter the realm of nonduality?" Manjusri says, "All explanations are dualistic. To my mind, in all dharmas there are no words, no preaching, no demonstration, and no recognition. It is beyond all questions and answers. That is entering the dharma gate of nonduality."

Then Manjusri asks Vimalakirti, "Each of us has spoken. Now tell us, good man, what is the bodhisattva's entry into the dharma gate of nonduality?"

"What will Vimalakirti say?" Setcho asks in the koan.

What do you think? How will he answer? The sutra tells us, "Vimalakirti kept silent, without saying a word." Then Manjusri praises him, saying, "Good, good. Not to have even syllables or words is truly entering the dharma gate of nonduality." Even here, Manjusri has to use words.

Vimalakirti's sitting is not just sitting in silence, not just quietism. This is one of the key points of the koan. His silence has been traditionally described as a dynamic Silence, "the thundering silence of Vimalakirti." It is not silence at all but a great, thundering dharma ROAR! In the history of Zen there have been many paintings of this famous scene. Hakuin did a fine portrait of the wily old Vimalakirti, a kind of companion piece to his many excellent portraits of Bodhidharma. Take a close look at it sometime. You can find a reproduction in D. T. Suzuki's classic, *Manual of Zen Buddhism.* There's Vimalakirti, alive and well.

Engo's afterword or appreciatory word is as follows: "What folly! That aged old Yuima, grieving that he had been born distressed in mind, lying there in Vaisali, his whole body withered and exhausted. When the patriarch teacher of the seven buddhas"—that's Manjusri—"came, he thoroughly tidied up his sickroom and earnestly asked about the entrance to the one and only." The "one and only" is the realm of nonduality. "But that gate had already been broken down. And even if it had not been broken down, when the golden-maned lion visited him, it would not have found him."

Manjusri is often portrayed in Buddhist iconography astride a golden lion that represents the vigor and majesty of the dharma. In his right hand he holds a delusion-cutting sword. In his left he holds a sutra book. His hair is usually in five sets of curls or braids to represent the five wisdoms. He is usually seated on the Buddha's right. On the left there might be Samantabhadra, the bodhisattva of compassionate action. These two, Manjusri and Samantabhadra, are the right and the left arm of the Buddha. One is wisdom, the other com-

passion. Without both, the Buddha is a cripple. Without the wisdom and vigor of Manjusri, the Buddha's Samantabhadra-like compassion can become mere sentimentality. Conversely, without the
compassion of Samantabhadra, Manjusri's lionlike vigor and wisdom
can become cold and abstract.

In a life of Oneness there are no barriers, no gates. The whole universe fits easily into a ten-foot-square room, with no diminution at
all. Intrinsically, the only gates are the ones we erect ourselves. Zen
training is nothing more nor less than demolishing these self-created
barriers so that we can at last finally reenter the place we never really
left. "What could be more wonderful!" as Yasutani-roshi says in *The
Three Pillars of Zen* in speaking about the koan Mu. At the moment of
Awakening, we see that the gate was broken down long ago. We
see, in truth, that it never existed at all.

Continue to question, question, looking deeply, steadfastly into
your koan. Or pay attention to each breath, if that is your practice.
Or stay fully engaged with the practice of pure attention—*shikantaza*,
pure sitting. Stay with your practice, whatever its form. The gate
of nonduality swings open. As the *Mumonkan* implies—for *Mumonkan*
means "gateless gate"—it is a gateless barrier. Realize this. Then you
can have your own lively dialogue with the old layman of Vaisali,
eye to eye. What will Vimalakirti say? What will Vimalakirti say?

5

Bodhisattva Fu Lectures
on the Diamond Sutra

BLUE CLIFF RECORD, CASE 67

Emperor Wu of Liang asked the great Bodhisattva Fu to expound the *Diamond Sutra*. Fu mounted the platform, struck the lectern with his baton, and descended from the platform. The emperor was dumb-founded. Master Chih said to him, "Does your majesty understand?" The emperor replied, "No, I do not understand at all." Master Chih said, "The great bodhisattva has expounded the sutra thoroughly."

VERSE

> Instead of staying in his hut
> He stirred up dust in Liang.
> Had Chih not lent a hand,
> He would have had to leave the country,
> As Bodhidharma did, by night.

The actors in this drama are Emperor Wu, Fu Daishi, and Maha-sattva Chih. Emperor Wu also appears, equally nonplussed, in an-other koan, the very first in the *Blue Cliff Record*, with Bodhidharma. He asks Bodhidharma about the first principle of Buddhism. Bodhidharma answers, "Vast emptiness, no holiness." Most likely the emperor's jaw dropped. He had been busy building temples and supporting the teachings. He was expecting a good word about all the merit, or good karma, he was acquiring. So he responds, "Who are you standing before me?" That is: If there's no holiness, who are you? Aren't you a great sage? Aren't you a holy man? Bodhidharma, uncompromising as ever, answers most directly, "I don't know."

Emperor Wu had been a soldier, actually a local commander. Infighting among the ruling clans had led the nation to chaos. He took action and finally assumed control, becoming emperor himself around 470. After he had taken the throne he had new commentaries made on the five Confucian classics, and he liked to expound on them. He seems to have been an ardent Taoist, and was said to have been a very filial man. One day, as Thomas Cleary puts it in the introduction to his translation of the *Blue Cliff Record*, the emperor thought of attaining the transmundane teaching in order to requite his parents' kindness. And so he abandoned Taoism and began practicing Buddhism. He received the bodhisattva precepts, put on Buddhist vestments, and expounded wisdom teachings to recompense his parents.

At this time the Mahasattva Master Chih was confined in prison. While in prison it is said that he reproduced his body and wandered around, teaching in the city. The emperor found out about this and was inspired. After this he esteemed Chih highly and so, one assumes, had him released from prison. Master Chih had a way of disappearing and appearing in an incomprehensible manner. A most extraordinary fellow.

Fu Daishi was one of the most remarkable laymen in Buddhism. Miraculous stories abound about his life. In fact, he is one of the three outstanding lay practitioners most highly regarded in the entire history of Buddhism. There were, of course, others whose lives never made it into the records. Perhaps they didn't have this same archetypal power, and stories didn't coalesce around them. Then again, we know today that for less worthy reasons most of the great women practitioners disappeared from the official records as well.

The first of the "great three," going all the way back to the time of the Buddha, was Vimalakirti, the wealthy householder who, spiritually speaking, seems to have arrived at the Buddha's own lofty level. Then there are Fu Daishi, who lived from 497 to 569, and Layman P'ang, who comes several hundred years later, around 740, toward the end of the T'ang era. Important koans focus on each of these great lay figures.

The word *daishi* is a Japanese term which, depending on the characters, has several meanings. In this case, *dai* means "great" and *shi* means "virtuous teacher." It is said that Fu Daishi was kindly as a youth, and that he was a fisherman. The records say that when he had filled his basket with fish he would put it in the deep part of the river, saying, "Those who want to go, go; those who want to stay, stay." (You can find this in the out-of-print classic *Zen Dust*, from which much of this biographical information is taken.)[1] People in his village, it is also said, thought him somewhat daft. At sixteen he married, and he and his wife had two sons. When he was about twenty-four, he was sitting on a riverbank fishing when a monk came along and spoke to him about the teachings of the Buddha. Perhaps he talked to him about the first Buddhist precept, not to kill but to cherish all life. In any case, Fu must have been deeply moved by the talk, for when he looked into the water and saw his reflection, there was a nimbus of light around his shoulders and head. Perhaps this is a symbolic way of saying that he had had an awakening. After this he threw away his poles and nets and changed his life, never fishing again. Instead he made the salvation of others his chief aim.

He built a little hut for himself and his family between a pair of sala trees at the foot of nearby Pine Mountain. It was between two sala trees that the Buddha had entered parinirvana, and perhaps Fu chose this site because it reminded him of the Buddha's own life. Later, when Fu had attained deep enlightenment, he took a religious name meaning "the bodhisattva who would attain emancipation between the twin sala trees." By day he and his wife worked in the fields or hired themselves out as laborers. At night he sat in zazen or spoke about the dharma to anyone interested in listening. For seven years he undertook ascetic disciplines. There is no mention of what

these were, but afterward it is recorded that, as a result of his practices, he had had visions in which three buddhas appeared to him.

When I was living in a monastery in Rangoon, we were required
to sleep on a solid wood plank bed that had a very thin grass mat on
it. One time I told one of the head monks there about sitting in full
lotus while training in Japan, and he said that that was asceticism.
"In Burma," he said, "we sit half-lotus." This was considered to be
the standard way to sit; to the Burmese, the full lotus looked like
asceticism. "What about sleeping on this hard plank bed?" I asked.
"Isn't that asceticism?" "No, that's natural, that's the way everybody
sleeps here." When I got back to Japan I told the Japanese monks that
the Burmese monk said sitting full lotus is asceticism and that sleeping on a solid plank bed is not. They laughed. "It's just the opposite,"
they insisted. "Sitting full lotus is natural. Sleeping on a plank is asceticism." In Japan, monks sleep on a futon, not a very thick one,
what they call a *senbei* futon. A *senbei* is a thin cracker. One person's
asceticism is another person's indulgence!

These visions in which three buddhas appeared to Fu Daishi are
most interesting. Many of the great masters have had visions at one
time or another. They are not what we call *makyo*—delusional or ob-
structive hallucinations. Perhaps we might say makyo are temporary
states that appear if one is straining oneself or out of balance. The so-
called higher types of makyo, such as speaking in tongues or regress-
ing to past lifetimes, usually appear when the upper levels of the
mind become quiet and deeper material comes up to consciousness.
But visions seem to be something else. Dreams and visions also differ
from each other. Dreams usually involve things that are personal to
the dreamer; visions have a more universal element.

After Fu Daishi's vision, a local district official thought him possessed and had him imprisoned without food or water in order to
cure him. Ten days later, when the official went to see the Daishi, he
found him well and in good spirits. The amazed official released him.
Many students gathered around him. He began to say that he had
come from the Tushita Heavens, where the future Buddha, Maitreya,
is preparing to be born, millions of years from now. There was a fam-

ine in his district, and the Daishi sold his house and fields and used the money to feed starving villagers. He even persuaded his wife and sons, as well as a number of other persons, to be sold as slaves to raise money for this same purpose. Later they were all freed by the landowner who had bought them, so it may have been a symbolic purchase. In the year 534 the Daishi dispatched a disciple with a letter setting forth his religious views to Liang Wu, the emperor of our koan. Later the emperor commanded the Daishi to appear before him. He was much impressed and ordered Fu Daishi to live near the capital so he might continue having audiences with him.

Many eminent monks now came to the Daishi's gate, and the emperor summoned him for several more audiences. In 535, however, the Daishi returned to his old home and built a Buddha hall and a pagoda among the sala trees there. In the early spring of 548, the Daishi gave away all his fields and estates to the people (evidently he had become a man of some means). The next month he told his followers that he was going to go without food to purify his body and mind, and that on the eighth day of the fourth month—that is, April 8, the Buddha's birthday—he would immolate himself as an offering to the three treasures of Buddha, dharma, and sangha, and for the benefit of all living creatures on earth. He hoped thus to bring to an end the suffering the people were undergoing as a result of the many military disasters at that time. When the day of his immolation came, nineteen of his disciples wanted to burn themselves in his place. A hundred or more, it is said, actually burned their fingers, cut off their ears, or sold themselves as slaves. Others engaged in other extreme ascetic practices to persuade the Daishi not to carry out his intention. He finally yielded to their pleas.

During the Vietnam War, a number of Buddhist monks immolated themselves as an ultimate way of protesting the war. The most dramatic case was that of a monk who did so while seated in zazen. The photograph of that burning monk was seared into the mind of everyone who saw it, and it remains one of the most powerful images to have emerged from the sixties. (It is said that the monk's heart did not burn and that it is still enshrined in one of the pagodas in Vietnam.) At the time of that burning I was giving public talks on Zen, and invariably the subject would come up of the immolation of these Vietnamese monks. What kind of teaching is Buddhism, people asked, that it teaches you to burn yourself? Why are they doing this? Doesn't Buddhism cherish human life at all?

The people who asked these questions were clearly very upset. Yet this was not suicide. It was a heroic attempt to reach the heart of the American people and to relieve the terrible suffering of the Vietnamese people. And indeed, the psychic shock it caused may have considerably shortened the war. At the time, Yasutani-roshi read that certain Japanese Buddhist periodicals had criticized this monk for burning himself. They said his act had given Buddhism a bad name. Yasutani-roshi wrote a letter to the editor in response, saying that before these people criticized the monk's action, they should try to burn just the tip of their little finger. Then, after they had done that, they might be more qualified to make a meaningful statement on this particular incident.

During the years after the Daishi agreed not to immolate himself, he continued to care for the poor. He regularly held religious meetings (we might assume this would mean zazen, teishos, and chanting) to prevent misfortunes and continued to purify his mind and body through zazen as well as through ascetic practices, to bring peace and ease to all living beings. He died May 25, 569, at the age of seventy-three. Many, it is said, considered him to have been an incarnation of Maitreya. He had never taken formal vows and orders but had remained a layman his whole life. He was portrayed in paintings and sculptures with his wife and boys—a tall, thin figure with a long beard wearing a Confucian hat, a Buddhist robe, and Taoist shoes. He was clearly seen as someone who had harmonized China's three great spiritual traditions. He is also credited with the invention of the revolving bookcase, which, like the prayer wheel, was to help those who turned it attain salvation, or at least better karma, no matter how ignorant they might be.

Several of the so-called preliminary koans have been attributed to him. These are koans that one works on to "get one's legs," so to speak, before beginning work on the *Mumonkan* and *Hekiganroku*. One reads, "Empty-handed yet holding a hoe; walking yet riding a water buffalo." Another is, "Standing on a bridge. Lo, the bridge flows and the water does not."

Our final protagonist in this koan is the *Diamond Sutra* itself, one of the most highly esteemed texts in Zen. At least half a dozen koans are taken from, or relate directly to, the *Diamond Sutra*. A famous line from the *Diamond Sutra*, "Past mind is not attainable, present mind is not attainable, future mind is not attainable," is utilized with great spontaneity and skill by the old teahouse woman who skewers the *Diamond Sutra* expert, Tokusan, in a famous mondo that forms the commentary to koan number twenty-eight in the *Mumonkan*, "Ryutan Blows Out a Candle." The old woman was selling cakes, known colloquially as "mind-refreshers." Tokusan, hungry and tired, stopped to refresh himself. She saw the big pack he carried on his back and asked what he was toting around, what it contained. "Commentaries on the *Diamond Sutra*," he replied loftily. The old woman said, "Oh, I have heard that in the *Diamond Sutra* it says, 'Past mind is not attainable, present mind is not attainable, future mind is not attainable.' Tell me, venerable monk, just which mind do you intend to refresh?" Tokusan, as yet unenlightened, was stuck. His pride fell; humble now, he asked if there might be a Zen master nearby. In this way he came to his teacher, Ryutan.

"The *Diamond Sutra* and Being Reviled" forms case ninety-seven in the *Hekiganroku*. It goes like this: "The *Diamond Sutra* says, 'One who is reviled by others has done wicked acts in former lifetimes which doom him to fall into evil worlds, but because of the scorn and vilification by others in the present life, the transgressions in the former life are wiped out.'" Like this koan, the *Diamond Sutra* is profound, brief, and very concentrated. The Sixth Patriarch, when just a boy hauling firewood to support his old mother, heard this sutra being chanted by a wandering monk and had an initial awakening. Tradition holds that the monk was chanting the line "Arouse the mind without its abiding anywhere."

A core teaching of the *Diamond Sutra* (or *Diamond Cutter*, as it is sometimes called, because its wisdom is so concentrated that, like a diamond, it cuts everything while nothing cuts it) consists of a series of brief exchanges between the Buddha and his disciple Subhuti on the nature of Truth. Here is section 22 in its entirety:

> Then Subhuti asked Buddha: "World-Honored One, in the attainment of the consummation of incomparable enlightenment did Buddha make no acquisition whatsoever?"
>
> Buddha replied: "Just so, Subhuti. Through the consummation of incomparable enlightenment I acquired not even the least thing; wherefore it is called 'consummation of incomparable enlightenment.' "[2]

According to certain scholastic schools, simply turning this scripture of twenty-odd pages is called "upholding the scripture." Fu Daishi's revolving bookcase was designed to serve this meritorious end. According to the scholastic schools, the scripture itself has great spiritual power, and imprinting its verses on the mind awakens the mind to its own innate wisdom. Another master said, "Realizing buddhahood is called 'upholding the scripture.' " The Diamond Sutra also says that all the buddhas have complete and perfect awakening, and that they come forth from this scripture.

To return to the koan, Emperor Wu of Liang asked Fu Daishi to give a lecture on the Diamond Sutra. The background to this koan states that the emperor had actually asked Chih to lecture on the Diamond Sutra for an audience of dignitaries. But Chih said that he was not the one to do it; the person to give such a talk was Fu Daishi. And so Fu Daishi was summoned.

Picture the scene. All the distinguished and powerful guests are there in their finest robes. The emperor is seated on his throne in full regalia. Everybody is expecting to hear a brilliant, deeply spiritual lecture by the greatest living authority on the Diamond Sutra. They won't have to do anything but just sit there and listen, and their minds will open. The Daishi mounts the platform. His listeners lean forward, ready to catch his every word. Suddenly he strikes the platform with his baton—*Crack!*—and descends from the platform once again. The emperor is dumbfounded. Poor Emperor Liang; he must have had some pretty bad karma to run up against both Bodhidharma and Fu Daishi! He had asked Fu Daishi to give a lecture on the sutra, which teaches that there is no teaching and no learning, and Fu Daishi responded brilliantly. Of course, to truly know that there is no teaching and no learning is to know a great deal. There he is, that eccentric figure in his Confucian hat, Buddhist robes, and Taoist shoes. *Crack!* Master Chih asks, "Does your majesty understand?" The emperor replies, "No, I do not understand."

In the first koan in the *Blue Cliff Record*, the emperor had encountered Bodhidharma and was asked by Chih, "Does your majesty know who this man is?" "I do not know," answered the emperor. (Is this the same sort of "I don't know" that Bodhidharma himself used when asked by the emperor, "Who are you?") Chih said, "He is the Bodhisattva Avalokiteshvara transmitting the Buddha Mind Seal."

Now Chih says, "The great bodhisattva has expounded the sutra thoroughly." Neither Master Chih nor the Daishi are putting the emperor on. It's not a trick. Everything is truly in that one *Crack!* But did he really expound the sutra? After all, the sutras express the heart, the spirit of the Buddha's dharma. Was all *that* in *Crack!*? Can it really be?

Or we may ask, "Where is Fu Daishi right now?"

Crack!

There he is, preaching the unattainable dharma thoroughly and clearly.

Do you hear him?

6

Layman P'ang's Beautiful Snowflakes

A question that comes up in dokusan from time to time is whether working on koans involves, in the end, just another kind of thinking. Isn't a spiritual inquiry like "What is Mu?" just adding another thought to the bundle of thoughts one is already carrying around in one's head, and so impeding the attainment of a deeper state of concentration?

"Joshu's Mu" is the first koan in the most famous koan collection, *The Gateless Barrier* or *Mumonkan*, compiled by the monk whose spiritual name, taken from his deep insight into the koan Mu, was Mumon. He lived from 1183 to 1260. If koans are used by a Zen teacher in training students, the *Mumonkan* is the collection that those students will work on first.

The case reads as follows: "Once a monk asked Joshu, 'Does a dog have buddha nature?'" Joshu, the famous Chinese Zen master whose lips were said to flash light—that is, whose every word glowed with inner truth—answered "Mu." Literally, *Mu* means "no" or "not." The inquiry "What is Mu?" is the core, or the gripping question, of the koan. The sutras, the recorded words of the Buddha, say that all beings, even insects, plants, and worms, possess buddha-nature. Why, then, did Joshu, a deeply learned as well as a deeply enlightened Zen master, answer "No" or "Not"? Fundamentally, the question becomes, "What is Mu?" or simply, "Mu?!"

When we talk about thoughts, we are usually referring to the ceaseless flow of random thoughts in and out of the mind, rather than focused and incisive thinking. But in Zen Buddhism we use the term *one thought* to indicate that in Zen practice the mind is honed to a condition of complete absorption in only one thing—Mu, in this case. Using the mind in this focused, concentrated way is a conscious exertion and ultimately a deeply creative, liberating act. It is a purposeful aiming of the mind through thought and then beyond thought. Through such focusing the world comes alive. Just Mu! and the bird sings, the encouragement stick (*kyosaku*) cracks! The garbage truck rumbling outside the window swallows trash with a roar and a crash! Just Mu, just "one thought," and we emerge from the "pale cast of thought," as Hamlet would say, like a butterfly from a cocoon. Out we come into the vividly new, yet completely ordinary and familiar world. The realm of "one thought" is vast and wide. No irrelevant, idle thoughts churn there, and no sticky conceptions and notions grab and cling.

However, because of the habitual power of sticky, deep-seated notions, certain individuals may experience a failure of will, or even a will to failure. There are people who are earnestly practicing—it doesn't matter whether they're working on a koan or not—who can reach a certain point and with no warning at all, their mind is suddenly overcome with the feeling that they can never succeed. They've failed so often in so many other activities, they tell themselves, that Zen is bound to end up as another failure. Why make a supreme effort?

What *can* be done? Wholehearted zazen is the path of freedom. Apply yourself minute by minute to your practice—whether it's counting the breath, following the breath, *shikantaza*, or absorption in a koan. This sustained exertion, as Zen Master Dogen called it, will see you through.

Of course, all kinds of rationalizations can interfere with pure effort: Enlightenment isn't worth it. I know enlightened people who seem no better than anyone else. The effort is too painful. Why go on? It's too much to ask of myself. Or, What if I do come to kensho? So what? What difference can it make? I'll have to sit even more and work on all those other difficult koans. Or if you are experiencing pain in your foot or your leg or back or neck, you may feel, If I try hard now I might do permanent damage. I'd better ease off or quit.

There may be a deep pattern at work here. Perhaps in life you find this same process replayed: you make a strong start in a certain direction, reach a kind of high point, then various rationalizations set in, and the whole enterprise collapses. It might be subtler, less dramatic. The exertion itself can just become habitual, mechanical, without real life and immediacy in it.

Old habits of mind run deep. Even with a strong desire to really accomplish worthwhile things, your energy can still find negative channels in which to settle. You can be your own—always successful—prophet of doom. When things go sour, you won't have to blame yourself because you can always say, See? It's just as I said; I'm a failure. It's a way of taking yourself off the hook, and as a strategy for survival, it provides a certain amount of security and predictability in an unsafe, unsure world. The unknown can be frightening. Ironically, then, the fear of failure itself and of the pain it might cause can breed an attachment to failure and undercut your best efforts. But by practicing, by coming to sesshin, you have already announced that you have outgrown all such unreliable routes to happiness. You have already acknowledged that they do not work—in fact, that they are self-defeating, and so cannot work.

When inner obstacles arise during sesshin, we can remember that we are not alone. We are all working together—the fifty or so other sitters, the monitors, and the teacher. In addition, the schedule has been honed to help us each fully focus all our energies and attention on the practice. We really have a golden opportunity! Oceans of untapped energy and waves of invisible support sustain us in ways impossible in the ordinary, daily, complex rounds of life. By making a moment-to-moment effort, sustained by this vast field of communal energy, little by little old frozen patterns of thought and emotion are transcended and then transformed. One may coast for brief periods, but by making use of all this help, one can avoid falling back under the sway of these patterns. The exertion of one person supports the exertions of everyone else. With all the encouragement, the deep stillness, and the silent help of the monitors and teacher, each participant has an unparalleled opportunity. Our little thoughts, our outgrown and limiting attitudes and perceptions, block huge amounts of energy and awareness. It's like a finger blocking the sun. The finger is tiny, yet it can keep the sun's light from our eyes. In sesshin you have the help you've yearned for and, perhaps, prayed for to remove such blocks. As William James says, "All religion begins with the cry 'Help!' " Use the help that is available in sesshin to accomplish your deep longing for awakening.

Remember, too, that habits of clinging always hang on a strong sense of "me" and "my." *I can't do it; I'm a failure.* Consciously or unconsciously, the focus is on the "I," on an old story with "me" at the center. Yet if one is really determined to go beyond this limited sense of "I," one can and will. Sesshin provides us with an unparalleled opportunity to awaken.

Of course there can be difficulties. At sesshin there are people who really motivate themselves. They work hard, sit a lot, stay focused during meals and breaks, and still can't seem to get beyond a certain barrier. They may have been to a number of sesshins and each time get stuck at the same point, sesshin after sesshin. What to do? they wonder.

The first thing such persons need to realize is that doing the sesshin the way they've always done it can only bring them, as always, to the same point. Why not change? If they typically use the break periods for rest, why not decide this sesshin to *not* rest at those times? Or if they have never stayed up longer than an hour or two past the end of the formal sitting, why not decide to stay up longer? If your energy has become dammed up in a certain pattern, strike off on a new path. Once you do, energy begins to flow and you can find yourself more concentrated and alive than ever, able to do things you couldn't do previously.

Conversely, if during sesshin you are accustomed to staying up most of the night, it might be well to try changing that too. Why not stay up, perhaps, just an hour or two, or until you feel sleepy, then go to bed? If you wake up later, get up and do zazen. If a real desire for awakening is present, breaking or transcending or leaving behind—however you want to describe it—your normal limits will naturally follow. Make a determination and follow it up with a dedicated effort. The inspiration as to what to change will come.

So much for these preliminary words on sesshin effort and the problems and limits one may face. Let us now examine koan number forty-two in the *Hekiganroku* or *Blue Cliff Record*, "Layman P'ang's Beautiful Snowflakes."

> When Layman P'ang took leave of Yakusan, the latter asked ten students to escort him to the temple gate to bid him farewell. The Layman, pointing to the falling snowflakes, said, "Beautiful snowflakes—they fall nowhere."
>
> "Where do the flakes fall, then?" asked one of the Zenkaku. The Layman slapped him.
>
> "Even a layman shouldn't be so crude," said the monk.
>
> "How can you call yourself a Zen monk?" cried the Layman. "Old Yama won't let go of you."
>
> "How about yourself?" said the monk.
>
> Whereupon the Layman gave him another slap and said, "You look but you are blind; you speak but you are mute."
>
> —*Blue Cliff Record*, Case 42

Then Setcho adds by way of commentary, "If I were him, I would have made a snowball and thrown it at him. Like this!" [Roshi demonstrates.] And that's the end of the koan.

Zenkaku, by the way, is a Japanese word that means simply "one who does Zen." We don't have a really suitable English equivalent. There are various words in Japanese to describe a practitioner of Zen. But the word *practitioner* has no *Zen* in it. *Student* isn't exactly right, having too much of the midnight oil about it.

Yakusan was a famous Chinese Zen master. His Chinese name was Yueh-shan Wei-yen, and he lived from 745 to 828. In Japanese he's called Yakusan Igen. His biography, as it is presented in *Zen Dust*,[1] relates that at seventeen he had his head shaved by a monk who was a disciple of the famous Nangaku Nan-yueh. Then until the age of twenty-nine, when he took full ordination, he devoted himself to the study of the Vinaya, or codes of behavior, as well as the sutras, that is, the written teachings. In 773 Igen visited the famous Zen master Sekito Kisen. On Sekito's advice he then went to see the great Matsu (Baso), and remained with him, training diligently, for a number of years. Still, he later returned to serve Sekito and receive dharma transmission from him. Then, before Sekito's death, he left Mount Nangaku for Yakusan, in present Hunan province. (*San*, by the way, means "mountain.")

It is said that when Igen first arrived on the mountain, he asked the local village headman if he would let him have a cowshed to live in. Later, when his assembly of disciples grew larger, a hut was built for him. Yakusan, as he was called (after the mountain on which he lived), now a teacher, continued his sutra study, examining such central texts as the *Avatamsaka-sutra*, the *Mahaparinirvana-sutra*, and the *Saddharmapundarika-sutra* (*Lotus Sutra*) in the light of his own enlightenment and advanced Zen practice. Interestingly, he disapproved of sutra study for his monks.

In the summer of 820, Ri Ko, the prefect, or governor, of nearby Roshu came to pay his respects, and a famous mondo took place. When the governor entered Yakusan's room, the master was holding a volume of sutras and did not look up. His attendant said, "Master, the prefect is here." Still Yakusan continued with his study. Ko, the governor, said disparagingly, "To hear the name is better than to see the face"—a well-known Chinese expression.

"Prefect!" instantly exclaimed the master.

"Yes, your reverence," responded Ko.

Yakusan demanded, "How dare you esteem the ear and scorn the eye?"

At once Ko bowed, hands held palm to palm, and offered apologies. He now asked, "What is the Tao?"

With his hand, the master pointed up and then down. "Do you understand?" he asked.

"No," admitted Ko, "I do not understand."

"The clouds are in the heaven, the water is in the jar," said the master.

There is a famous Zen ink-painting from China that shows this encounter taking place outdoors. The master is seated at a stone table. Ko is standing, palms together before him. Clouds are overhead, and a vase with flowers is on the table before the master. A box of sutra scrolls also rests on the stone slab tabletop.

Ko, delighted with these words, bowed deeply and offered this verse:

He has trained his body to resemble that of a crane.
Beneath a thousand old pine trees are two boxes of sutras.
I came to ask about Tao; there were only these words:
"The clouds are in the heaven, the water is in the jar."[2]

Then, it is said, Ko asked, "What are the precepts, meditation, and prajna?" In other words, what are the crucial things that characterize the religious life: moral and ethical codes, methods of realization, and practice? What is realization, or wisdom?

The master responded, "My room is empty of all such useless furnishings."

Ko, it seems, could not readily grasp the profound implication of these words. He must have looked puzzled, perhaps even dismayed. No precepts? No forms of meditation? No wisdom? The master was compassionate. Noticing his distinguished disciple's befuddlement, he continued, "Prefect, if you wish to take on this thing, you must at once sit down upon the summit of the mountain high, high, and walk upon the bottom of the sea, deep, deep." So ends the mondo.

What do you understand to be the master's meaning in saying, "My room is empty of all such useless furnishings. Precepts, meditation, wisdom—none are here"? Clearly he is not saying that precepts, meditation, and wisdom are unnecessary. They are central to the religious life, the decent life, the ordinary life of one on the Way, and cannot be discarded. Yet Yakusan is not lying when he says that his room, his mind, is empty of all useless additions and furnishings. He is an accomplished interior decorator of the most refined sort. Yasu-tani-roshi spoke of precepts and lifestyle as the furnishings, zazen the foundation, and kensho, or awakening, the living space of the realized house.

To continue, one evening Yakusan, the master, walked to the top of the mountain. As the clouds parted and the moon appeared, Yaku-san suddenly laughed a great, resounding laugh. The sound echoed miles away. ("Ha ha ha ha ha!" laughed a contemporary layman whose enlightenment account is recorded in *The Three Pillars of Zen*. "There's no reasoning here at all! Ha ha ha ha ha!" That laugh lies at the heart of Zen.) Well, people gathered to investigate the matter of Yakusan's great laugh and came to Mount Yaku. The monks said, "Oh, it's just that last night the master laughed a great laugh on the top of the mountain." Later our friend the governor presented the master with the following poem:

He has chosen a lonely dwelling and is content
with the rustic life;
Year after year he goes to greet no one, he sees no one off.
Once he climbed straight to the top of a lone peak,
And, as the moon broke through the clouds,
laughed a great laugh.[3]

Many monks, nuns, and masters, especially in the great T'ang pe-riod, but also before and after, lived this kind of simple, dedicated life. They too laughed the great laugh. Their contribution to Zen is inestimable.

Yasutani-roshi, in an article that appeared in *Zen Bow* some years ago, said that masters living alone in the mountains, sitting a great deal in zazen with no visitors to receive or monasteries to administer, may generate great samadhi power, which has an invisible but pro-found influence on awakening the minds of countless people. He re-marks that people who remain on a purely material level could easily protest that this kind of activity has no social value whatever. Yet,

Yasutani-roshi insists, despite appearances, it can be altruism of the highest order.

Still, there are not many people, particularly these days, who can live such a life. In our culture, Thoreau did it and did it well. But even he didn't live his whole life by himself, and Walden Pond saw him for only a relatively brief time. This kind of life is one type of Zen activity, and it is certainly a great one, but there are many other kinds. Indeed, in Zen the image of the mud-spattered, dust-covered sage who lingers in the market, tirelessly extending a helping hand to all troubled and wearied sentient beings, is also very compelling. There is no one way. At one time, one way might be appropriate; at another time, a different kind. Each of us must do what we are best able to do and what our karma decrees.

So it would be a mistake to deprecate activity in the city and to elevate the hermetic life. There are no absolutes. It's romantic, actually, to think of living in a cowshed. Young people, particularly those seeking a way out of the confines of our culture, often seem to want to imitate this. But it is really only for people who are able to do it. It can be difficult. And it can be an eye-opener. When I was in Thailand, one of our members, who was at that time a Buddhist nun living there, wanted very much to take me out to the country to stay at the little farm of a man who was later to become her husband. So we went out by boat to this place, where I slept right next to huge water buffaloes, magnificent animals, who lived in the cowshed. What happened? I came down with a terrible fever! Perhaps I didn't get it from staying there. I could just as easily have gotten the fever from drinking water earlier in a beautiful temple. But certainly the stay with the buffalo, although it was a memorable experience, didn't help my condition at all.

Here's another mondo involving Yakusan. When he was about to die he called out in a loud voice, "The Dharma Hall is falling down! The Dharma Hall is falling down!" The monks rushed to hold up the pillars. The master clapped his hands and laughed loudly. "You don't understand!" he exclaimed, and thereupon passed away. He was in his eighty-fourth year. He was a vigorous man and probably cried out in such a loud voice that the monks didn't realize he was speaking about himself.

Now let us say something about Layman P'ang, or Ho Koji (*koji* being the Japanese term for layman), as he is widely known in Japan. There's a book on the life of P'ang put together by a group of people working under the direction of Ruth Fuller Sasaki, Yoshitaka Iriya, and Dana Fraser that is very much worth reading. It is titled *A Man of Zen: The Recorded Sayings of Layman P'ang*, and much of this background information is drawn from it.[4]

P'ang's full name was P'ang Yun, a Zen name meaning "lofty interior." His nickname, Tao-hsuan, meant "Way mystery." The exact date of his birth is not recorded but is said to have been around the year 740. He was married and had both a son and a daughter. His daughter, Ling-chao, whose name means "spirit shining," had a deep understanding of Zen. She and her father seem to have had a particularly close relationship. In middle age, P'ang, in one of the most famous and highly revered events in Chinese spiritual history, gave away his house and sank all his wealth and possessions in a river. This straightforward act caught the imagination not only of the Chinese people of his own day, but of Zen students ever since. It seems to have been his dramatic way of saying not only that such "useless furnishings" were unnecessary, but that they might even be harmful. He didn't want them tainting others. So, rather than just give them away, he dumped them in the river. It may have also been his way of jolting the minds of others into the realization that their own attachments to such things were misguided. It was the start of a mondo, the opening shot in a possible dialogue on the nature of attachment. Did anyone respond to his vivid presentation? How did his wife feel about it? Was she in accord with his view?

I remember discussing the matter of P'ang's renunciation with Ruth Sasaki years ago while I was in Japan. She was incensed that P'ang had ignored the needs of his wife and children. She saw it as short-sighted. Why, she wondered, hadn't he given his wealth to the poor? These are complex and personal questions that need to be looked at on an individual basis.

Sometimes people react this way when they hear of an Indian swami who renounces his family or of the Buddha's "great renunciation," because *renounce*, unfortunately, sounds a lot like *denounce*. *Renunciation* all too easily acquires a pejorative meaning in our minds. Renouncing one's family seems heartless. However, in almost all cases that I personally know of, not only were financial arrangements made to take care of the family, but ongoing and congenial communication was never sundered. Still, one can never be sure about the emotional effects of such a decision, whatever the finances may be. And such actions usually take place within a culture in which this kind of commitment to the spiritual quest is recognized and respected from the start.

So let's not think of these happenings as abandonments in the ordinary sense. It is often an arrangement made to enhance practice and teaching. Here it seems as though the father and the daughter went off in one direction and the mother and the son in another, although they were, it appears, all good friends. The father and the daughter, as well as the mother and the son, must have had a special affinity with each other and so got along well together. P'ang and his daughter made a meager living by making and selling bamboo utensils.

At all events, after disposing of his possessions, P'ang traveled to the mountain of Nan-yueh to visit the great Ch'an Master Shih-t'ou, by whom he was enlightened. Actually he had several enlightenment experiences. He also journeyed to meet the great Master Ma-tsu, and under Ma-tsu experienced great enlightenment, remaining afterward among the hundreds of disciples assembled there to become a dharma heir of that noted master. The mondo that led to his great enlightenment is a famous one and merits recounting. P'ang asked, "What is it that transcends all things in the universe?" The master answered, "When you have drunk up all the waters of the East River in a single gulp, I'll tell you."

A famous Zen verse attributed to Layman P'ang came out of his enlightenment; in it he reminds us that his everyday life is nothing special, declaring that all his miraculous power and supernatural activity are nothing other than drawing water and hauling firewood.

(Remember, there can be many enlightenments, and usually a first kensho is shallow compared to later ones.)

P'ang had attained to an ordinariness of the most profound sort. For him the daily events of life were miracles. Drawing water to wash and cook with, hauling firewood to prepare food and keep warm—aren't these truly amazing activities? So too, how is it that we can eat and digest our food? How is it that we think? How do we move our arm to lift the phone or our fingers to type at the computer keyboard? Who commands these actions? What miraculous being is it that wields such amazing powers? Not a day goes by in which miracles are not performed for those who have the eyes to see and the ears to hear.

After being guided to liberation by Ma-tsu, one of the most noted teachers of the great T'ang era—known as the Golden Age of Zen—P'ang went on pilgrimages in central China, matching his own Ch'an (the Chinese term for Zen) understanding against all comers—monks, masters, laypeople. Some of these exchanges, or mondo, have become koans. P'ang also wrote a number of poems whose central themes were Buddhist teaching, practice, and enlightenment, in addition to warnings of the pitfalls of the path.

Toward the end of his life Layman P'ang headed north, accompanied by his beloved daughter, Ling-chao. They lived in a cave near Deer Gate Mountain, where many famous poets resided. They had been there a few years when P'ang had his daughter prepare hot water, then took a bath, donned his robe, sat in the lotus posture, and said: "Tell me when the sun reaches high noon." His daughter watched and reported, "The sun has just reached noon, but its brilliance is eclipsed." P'ang went to see for himself. Thereupon his daughter sat down in the lotus posture and passed away. Her father returned, saw her, and exclaimed: "I spoke of it earlier, but now I'll have to do it later." He let seven days pass in which he may have performed Buddhist funeral services—seven being the usual number of days for such rites, which may extend for as many as forty-nine days—then passed away himself. This was certainly a remarkable way for them to die, with utter acceptance, absolutely no fear, and perfect understanding between them.

That is the background of our dramatis personae for this koan. P'ang and Yakusan were good dharma friends. They had practiced together for a long time. Layman P'ang had been visiting the temple—perhaps he was in residence for the traditional three-month training period—and was taking leave. Master Yakusan asked a group of laymen and Zen students, monks probably, to see P'ang to the temple gate, which may have been half a mile or so from the temple complex itself. We can well imagine that the master knew dharma combat would be the likely outcome—just as the Buddha did when he sent Manjusri to visit Vimalakirti. P'ang was known for his vigorous Zen style. Very likely, too, the monks who had been asked to go with P'ang were advanced in their spiritual training. So Master Yakusan was setting the ball rolling, creating a situation in which the dharma was likely to be revealed.

It is winter, and snow is falling. P'ang observes that the snow is very pretty as it comes down, yet truly there is no place where it can fall. This is his opening shot. The world of Zen is all around us. You can enter the gate anywhere, at any opportunity, if you are alert. P'ang is. And so, to begin a dharma duel, he offers this challenging statement. Sure enough, one of the members of the party picks up the gauntlet and responds, "Where do the flakes fall, then?" If they don't fall to the ground, where do they fall? P'ang slaps him. *Crack!* The starting point or first barrier to surmount in this koan is grasping the essence or spirit of Layman P'ang's falling snow. The second point is, what is the significance of that slap? Is it a rebuke? Is it a way of pointing something out? If so, what? Is it the answer the monk inquires after? To understand this, we will have to understand the spirit of the monk's initial response. Then the monk rebukes P'ang for being crude. Is he asking, Why did you do that? What did I say that called for that kind of a reaction on your part? Is he miffed? Or is his very ordinary response itself a challenge? Is he saying: Of course, but why are you being so dramatic?

P'ang counters, "How can you call yourself a Zen monk? Old Yama

won't let go of you!" Yama Raja—King Yama—is lord of the under-
world. Some say that his province is hell, but, strictly speaking, he's
neither in hell nor in heaven but rather in an indefinable place where
he keeps the huge book of karma that is the record of all people and
their thoughts and deeds. Looking up their karma, he assigns them
the proper place for their next rebirth. Or rather, he lets them look,
opening to the page that reveals the station and situation they have
themselves earned. "Old Yama won't let go of you," P'ang says. You
pretend to have some insight, but you're going to land in hell. You're
still stuck in birth and death.

The mood is challenging and very quick—like lightning. Yet there
is a playfulness here, too. Some translations seem to give the feeling
that there is anger or aggression in these exchanges, but that's never
the case in a true dharma exchange. There's never anger; you're never
trying to punish or denigrate anybody. There can, of course, be a
great deal of vitality and energy, for the obvious reasons: if there
weren't, the point would not be made. So these old-time Zen people
didn't hesitate to use their whole bodies and minds, to be fully engaged in each of their spiritual encounters. The normal rules of the
polite, hierarchical Confucian society no longer applied. No holds
were barred in such engagements of the spiritual life. And the point
was not to overcome so much as to *open*. So they slapped, they
pushed, all to drive home a point. Of course, to imitate this would
be mere buffoonery, and dangerous at that.

Presumably the monk who's been slapped has had some kind of
previous breakthrough. Why, then, does he respond as he does? Does
he fail to see the point? He answers, "How about yourself?" I'm not
so sure Yama's not going to let go of you either!

Suppose this monk had had really deep realization. What would
he have done then? What could he have done or said that would reveal that he was not a beginner? Would it have necessarily been any
different? This is yet another challenge the koan throws at us.

With that remark, the Layman gives him another slap and says,
"You look but you are blind; you speak but you are mute." Is this
second slap different from the first? In what way? And what does he

mean? Is P'ang saying that the monk can't see what's right in front of him? And what is there to see anyway, but the endless snow coming down? What is P'ang getting at? Is it an insult—a kind of authoritative, one-up verbal sting to go with the stinging rebuke of the slap?

In Zen there are different kinds of blindness, and degrees of blindness as well. There is the blindness before awakening and a blindness after awakening. There's the blindness of opening one eye and the blindness of having both eyes wide open. After enlightenment there's a blindness with a very positive implication—the blindness of seeing everything with the eye of equality, of being blind to the ordinary distinctions of the relative world. One doesn't see high or low, better or worse. One sees everything without a smudge of discrimination. There is a radiance, a real beauty, even within seeming ugliness. It's not simply that one ignores the ugliness or the suffering, but that one now sees, within it, wholeness and completeness. This is why it's said in Zen that a buddha is deaf, dumb, and blind, like the three proverbial monkeys. Yet even such blindness is not complete. It's only halfway.

P'ang says, "You speak but you are mute." You speak but you say wrong things. Or nothing, really, at all. You speak from a limited perspective. Let body and mind drop completely away! Speak without your tongue, without eyes, without a trace of self-consciousness. This, of course, would also imply that the monk would have to speak without any kind of anger, annoyance, or resentment. For annoyance, resentment, or anger would suggest that ego-clinging is still involved, and that the mouth, the eyes—indeed, all the senses—are still the gateways of the ego. The great Japanese Zen Master Bassui said that we are each born with these poisons of greed, anger, and delusion in our senses. How are we to live free of all this?

What would be a developed Zen person's way of doing this? Of looking at snow, for instance? What would be your way? The wily old layman not only engages the monks, he engages us. He buries us in snow.

Setcho, the compiler of this koan collection, presents a closing verse: "If I were him, I would have made a snowball and thrown it at him." Presumably "him" refers first to the monk and lastly to Layman P'ang—If I were the monk I would have hit P'ang with a snowball as soon as he opened his mouth. Perhaps if the monk had actually done that, P'ang would have been delighted. Absolutely delighted.

In what way would that have met the point, or points, of this koan? To know what to do, we must know what's involved. We must know the principle that's being so vividly demonstrated by this koan. "Beautiful snowflakes—they fall nowhere." Where then do they fall? Wallace Stevens, a poet close to home, has his own way of telling us about it in "The Snow Man." Listen:

> One must have a mind of winter
> To regard the frost and the boughs
> Of the pine-trees crusted with snow;
>
> And have been cold a long time
> To behold the junipers shagged with ice,
> The spruces rough in the distant glitter
>
> Of the January sun; and not to think
> Of any misery in the sound of the wind.
> In the sound of a few leaves,
>
> Which is the sound of the land
> Full of the same wind
> That is blowing in the same bare place
>
> For the listener who listens in the snow,
> And, nothing himself, beholds
> Nothing that is not there and the nothing that is.[5]

PART THREE

Koans

of

Our

Lives

7

Goso's No Words or Silence

Goso said, "When you meet a man of the Way on the Way, do not greet him with words, do not greet him with silence. Now, tell me, how will you greet him?"

COMMENTARY

If you can answer Goso intimately you are to be congratulated. But if you can't, be alert in every aspect of your life.

VERSE

If you meet a master on the Way,
Greet him neither with words nor with silence.
Give him an uppercut,
And as for understanding, there'll be understanding at once.

Koan number thirty-six in the *Mumonkan* is sometimes called "Goso's No Words or Silence." It is also called "Meeting a Man of the Way on the Way." Goso Hoen (Wu-tsu Fa-yen in Chinese) lived from approximately 1024 to 1104. He left home rather late, at the age of thirty-five, to become a monk. First he studied the teachings of the Consciousness Only school. Growing dissatisfied with this, he eventually left to seek out a teacher who could transmit the buddha-mind. That is, he came to Zen. He studied with several noted teachers, becoming a dharma heir of Shutan Zenji (Shu-tan Ch'an-shih). After Shutan's death he lived on Yellow Plum Mountain, which 400 years earlier had been the home of the Fifth Patriarch. Goso, or Hoen, as he is also called, was said to have been straightforward and unassuming in manner and plain, even colloquial, in his teaching style. Sometimes he is said to have referred to himself as Uncle To of West River (To being his family name), or "the fellow who lives somewhere-or-other at the foot of East Mountain" (Yellow Plum Mountain was also known as East Mountain). Although he might have been plain and unassuming, he became a noted master with many students. When he was about to die he said, "For the rich man a thousand mouths are too few, and for the poor man one body is too much. Farewell." He was more than eighty years old at the time. The next morning at dawn, sitting in the full lotus posture, he quietly passed away.

Here is a portion of a teisho that that "fellow who lives somewhere-or-other" gave in old age: " 'Yesterday I found a certain passage and I wondered if I should bring it up before all of you. But as I am an old man, I have forgotten the whole thing entirely. For some time I thought about it, but it wouldn't come back to me.' He was silent for a moment. Then he said, 'I have forgotten, I have forgotten!' adding, 'There is a Mahayana *dharani* [mystical Sanskrit formula] named "The Wise Enlightening King." If you recite it, you remember what you have forgotten.' " Goso then recited the mantra AN-A-RO-ROKU-KEI-SHA-BA-KA and clapped his hands. "Ha, ha, ha! I remember! I remember! If you try to find a buddha, you can never see one. If you search for a patriarch, you will never meet one. The sweet melon is sweet to the root; the bitter melon is bitter to the root!"[1]

If you try to find a buddha you can't see one, and if you search for a dharma ancestor, you will never meet one. And if you exert yourself to be a good person, you'll never be one. There is a fine mondo between Nansen (Nan-chuan) and Governor Ri Ko, a famous layman. After a sesshin he attended, the governor of the province was about to return to his administrative offices when Nansen asked him, "When you get back to your office, how will you govern the people?" The governor immediately said, "With compassion and understanding." "In that case," responded Nansen, "every last one of them will suffer."

If you try to be a good person, a loving person, the very effort will undermine the result. To be truly good and loving is the outcome of a certain mind-quality, a certain harmony, poise, and equilibrium, a certain inner purity, if you will. In other words, when you remove the hindrances to the natural outflow of these qualities, which are your birthright, everyone's birthright, then you naturally become what the world would call good and loving and compassionate. People in our society are constantly told to be good and loving—to love their neighbors as they love themselves. Perhaps from a purely ethical point of view, this has value, but it is a superficial approach to the matter. And it is most difficult to achieve. In a sense it is looking backward. Analogously, if you try to find a buddha, you can never see one. If you search for a dharma ancestor, you will never meet one. The very effort clouds your vision.

"The sweet melon is sweet to the root; the bitter melon is bitter to the root." When you taste life's sweetness, it is thoroughly sweet. You encounter something bitter and it is thoroughly bitter! What sort of buddha were you searching for?

Now let us revert to the case. "When you meet a man of the Way on the Way, do not greet him with words, do not greet him with silence." "Words" refers to conceptual thinking, self-referential verbalizing. Silence, too, is a form of speaking, just as the whiteness of a page is as much a part of the design as the black letters. In the same way, commonplace silence stands against speaking, even as it is a form of speaking itself.

Actually, there are many kinds of silences. True silence is present when no thought is in your mind at all, not even about silence. If you're with somebody and there's absolutely nothing in your mind, it's almost impossible not to be one with that person. Anyone who truly lives this way has no need to try to practice good deeds or to avoid evil. He or she has no attachments to the mind, no attachments to the products of the mind or the body. The eyes see things, but there is no attachment to what is seen. Everything is heard, but there is no attachment to what is heard. Such a person's hearing is a kind of no-hearing. Such a one's seeing is a kind of no-seeing. Or you could say that person hears with the eyes and sees with the ears. All is empty, transparent.

How is it possible to greet somebody with neither words nor silence? Ah, that's the question. To be or not to be. In working on this koan in the dokusan room, one has to express one's freely working Zen. Only when you yourself attain this stateless state can you really properly respond to the essence of the koan. Not words. Not silence. What then?

"When you meet a man of the Way on the Way . . ."

Although this is talking about an enlightened person, it could refer to anybody. However, if it's an enlightened person, you don't want to engage in trivialities.

Many years ago I knew a professor who was considered to be quite eccentric. At the time I was young, and he was quite old. He used to ride around in the trolley cars. Perhaps a sweet old lady would be sitting next to him, and by way of trying to be nice she would say, "Good morning, professor. Isn't it a lovely day today?" Without a word he would take a little card out of his vest pocket—men wore vests in those days—and hand it to the woman. The card said something like, "Now, isn't that an original remark?" He used to act in this way with all manner of people, disdaining the ordinary courtesies. Many people were very offended. It's a wonder he lived as long as he did.

What is an original remark? Take a piece of music. You can hear the same piece of music over and over again until it becomes quite timeworn. Then a fine conductor plays that same piece and, suddenly, it sounds new. It comes alive. Why? Because that conductor has infused new energy into those old notes. And by infusing those notes with new energy, he's made something vital of it. It is fresh and alive and has the power to move us beyond the ordinary and mundane. In the Bible one of the prophets asks, "Shall these bones live?" It's a pertinent question for each of us, every day. How shall we infuse the old bones of our daily existence with *life*?

Do you begin to get a glimpse of what is involved here? One might say it isn't so much what we say as *how* we say it; whether all of us is in it, or whether it's just our mouth idly flapping. And the same thing may be said about silence. There is such a thing as a pregnant silence, a fluent silence, even an eloquent silence. There is nobody who is immune to the implied flattery of a truly receptive silence. When somebody's talking to you, you're listening absolutely rapt, as though it's the first time you've heard such a thing. Listening with rapt attention is a good test for spouses. Can a loving spouse listen to an oft-repeated joke or a well-worn story as if for the first time, as if it hasn't been already heard a hundred times before? It's a good test for children of aging parents and students of aging teachers, too. Silence can be creative. When you relive a story with another, even though you've heard it many times before, if you really allow yourself to enter into the listening, if you are fully present, it comes alive. Such listening is not a polite pretense. If you listen creatively each time, it *is* new. It's not just that the words are new. It's that you and the whole world are new at that moment—as each moment they truly are.

This brings up a related subject, expressive sounds. The Japanese use lots of them—grunts, intonations, squeaks. We do, too: Uh-huh, uh-oh, mm-hm, yup. Oy! Ugh! Tsk-tsk! Aha! Oh, my. Really? and the like are sounds that sustain a conversation, an engagement through words. In Japanese, there are also all kinds of wonderful murmurings, even little growls, so many sound-words that naturally signal your engagement with the conversation through your listening. To be able to be with another person in a complete and total way is to laugh when they laugh and to make all the sounds that express connection. And yet, oddly, if you're talking to a very old friend, there can be long silences too. The older the friendship, the more intimate the relation, often the longer the silences. These pregnant, fluent silences are eloquent and allow "the hearts to entwine," as a Japanese profes-

sor once expressed it to me. A little sentimental, perhaps, but beautifully put nonetheless. And so we see that there are silences with a
capital S and with a small s. There are speakings, and there are Speakings.

For Zen students, perhaps the most vivid expression of silence is
Vimalakirti's "thundering silence," the core of a famous scene in the
Vimalakirti Sutra and the implied subject of case number eighty-four in
the Hekiganroku, "Vimalakirti's Gate of Nonduality" (see chapter 4).
In it, Manjusri presses Vimalakirti to elucidate the teaching of the
entrance into the principle of nonduality. And Vimalakirti remains
silent, saying not a word.

It was a popular scene in the imagination of ancient China, and
many scroll paintings, wall paintings, and carvings remain that bring
it to life. Perhaps the artists and public equally relished the irony of
the wealthy layman outdoing all the bodhisattva monks!

One big difference between Chinese Zen Buddhism and earlier
classical Indian Buddhism lies in the economical genius of the Chinese
mind. The koans express this well. The great vistas and vast themes
of the sutras can be condensed into one expressive point.

Here is a Zen master's comment on our koan, "Meeting a Man of
the Way on the Way," as quoted by Shibayama-roshi in Zen Comments on the Mumonkan.[2] The monk says, "It is said that if one meets a
man of Tao or a man of the Way on the Way, one must not greet him
with words or with silence. I wonder how one should greet him."
This, by the way, is actually a very old saying. It didn't originate
with Goso. And the master's reply is, "I have seen through the three
thousand worlds." That is, seen through the whole universe and
through the monk too.

Another time when a Zen master was asked that same question,
this was the reply: "Have a cup of tea." In what way do these responses transcend the underlying trap of this koan? For every koan is
setting a trap, a verbal trap. Each koan is deliberately trying to suck
us into reasoning and verbalizing, into making mental abstractions,
the better that we may finally see the great folly of all that, the better

to see how unreal it all truly is, and the better to see what is, indeed, Real. This is the great genius of koan Zen.

"Have a cup of tea" is such a simple, direct expression. Such simple words. How would you utter them? Koans demand responses of us. They are an eternal dialogue, and they ask us to enter into direct conversation with them. They may give us certain clues, certain answers. But we have to create our own responses. It's not a question of words suiting the actions. The actions must be suitable, and then the words may come if they're needed.

Now we come to Mumon's commentary. "If you can answer Goso intimately, you are to be congratulated. But if you can't, be alert in every aspect of your life." To be alert in every aspect of your life may sound fairly obvious. Certainly Zen students need to be alert and aware at all times, but it's the *kind* of alertness that is the issue here. Do you remember the famous film of the great Japanese director Akira Kurosawa—*The Seven Samurai?* A wise old swordsman tests possible companions for a future battle by calling to them to approach through an open doorway. A young samurai is hidden inside the entrance, standing with a stick, ready to strike each who may enter. The first enters and, as he's struck, strikes back. A tie. The second instinctively blocks the oncoming blow with his sword, so that he is not hit at all. The third takes a step forward, then pauses at the threshold, laughs, and refuses to enter the doorway at all. Three different degrees of awareness.

Being aware and alert can mean observing what needs to be observed and doing what needs to be done. It need be nothing more dramatic than turning off a light when it needs to be turned off, or opening a door for someone when it needs to be opened and closing it when it needs to be closed. It could mean taking out the garbage, doing the laundry, or not leaving your shoes strewn about where other people may trip on them. It can mean not being habitually forgetful. "Doing nothing, but leaving nothing undone," as the old saying has it, implies a high degree of awareness indeed. A person who is habitually forgetful is a person whose mind is filled with thoughts.

There are many degrees of awareness. The highest degree would be awareness of the indivisibility of all life, all existence. Being aware also means being aware of your practice at all times. If you're working on the koan Mu, for example, be aware, stay focused, continue questioning, and when you're sitting in zazen, don't let your mind get caught up in mundane things. Even when you are not formally doing zazen, as long as you're not engaged in necessary mental activity, keep inquiring, What is Mu? What can it be? What is Mu in this situation? What is Mu in that situation? If Mu is just Mu, why don't I know what Mu is? Can there be anything outside of Mu? If the world were destroyed, would Mu be destroyed? Whatever it is that keeps the mind involved with the questioning, do it. Keep at it. This kind of persistent, gnawing questioning helps maintain awareness. And it makes a breakthrough possible for the person who really wants to get through, or see into Mu.

There have been many laypeople who have been very much engaged in the affairs of life, yet who have nonetheless come to deep enlightenment. All through the history of Zen we find such people. And we find them in our present time too. It requires a certain discipline, and this discipline means essentially a willingness to scruff off the nonessentials. As Thoreau says, "Simplify, simplify, simplify." You can't carry on Zen training really well if your life is too complex, too hectic. A complex life means a life filled with anxieties and helter-skelter impulses, a life without a genuine center. This does not mean you shouldn't get involved in projects that are part of your normal functioning, or hesitate to do important things in your life because they might interfere with your Zen practice. Please don't make that mistake! There are lots of things we need to do, and we should do them even though they may carry stress and difficulty. If they're important enough, then we do them as best we can. But there are so many unnecessary things we might be better off not doing. To put it bluntly—don't do those.

Then we have the verse:

If you meet a master on the Way,
Greet him neither with words nor with silence.

Give him an uppercut;
And as for understanding, there'll be understanding at once.

Hakuin's famous comment on this is, "I don't like those last two lines
at all. They are too Zen monkish." When I was working on this
koan, Yasutani-roshi said that no English translation he knew of had
gotten it quite right. Evidently it has been difficult to get a really
accurate English equivalent.

No matter. It's the spirit of this we need to get clear. Be direct,
go right to the point, and don't be either foolishly sentimental or special and show-offish. Honest sentiment is a fine thing, but sentimentality is a kind of sappiness. When there is directness, there are no
gaps. At that moment there is no thought of self or other. There is no
reasoning, no theorizing. What comes from the mind goes to the
mind, or, as the saying has it, what comes from the heart goes to the
heart, directly, without any detour. In other words, speak clearly,
speak purely. Purely means without equivocation and without
thought of self. But don't make sureness itself a cult or directness a
habit.

Confucius says, "If you know, say you know. If you don't know,
say you don't know"—in itself a very simple, direct statement. But
how many people can do this? Lots of people feel ashamed if they're
asked a question and don't know the answer. They find it hard to
simply admit, "Gee, I don't know." Contrariwise, there are people
who are inordinately modest and hesitate to come forward with
what they do know—which may be a great deal. When our Zen is
freely working, when we are fully engaged, neither inflating nor de-
flating ourselves, we know where we stand and don't hesitate to express ourselves. This is Zen. It doesn't mean being rude or crude. In
traditional Chinese modes of expression, we can often see a wonderful indirectness at work, in which there is ample room to suggest and
imply. In our own conversations, our relations with other people, we
don't need to obtrude ourselves. There's no need, when listening to
someone, to begin telling them about yourself—unless, of course,

they ask. If you listen, just listen, and if you're speaking, just speak. This is really giving the hardest blow you can give for freedom.

So the next time you meet somebody on the Way, don't give him or her an uppercut physically ("too Zen monkish," says Master Hakuin). Just let the person understand that you both understand. That you understand what? You understand everything and you understand absolutely nothing at all. What is there to understand? Without resorting to either words or silence, just clearly tell me that.

8

Dogo Expresses Condolences

BLUE CLIFF RECORD, CASE 55

One day in the neighborhood of Dogo's Temple of Chang-chou, death occurred in a certain home and Zen Master Dogo took his disciple Zengen to express their condolences to the family. During the visit Zengen, the disciple, tapped the coffin and asked, "Is he alive or dead?" Dogo answered, "I won't say alive, I won't say dead." Zengen said, "Why don't you say?" Dogo repeated, "I won't say. I won't say." On the way back to the temple Zengen again asked, "Please tell me clearly, Master, whether he is dead or alive. If you don't tell me, I'll hit you." The teacher said, "Hit me if you like, but I won't say." So Zengen hit him.

At length Dogo died and Zengen, still troubled by the question, went to see Sekiso, a well-known Zen teacher. He told Sekiso how years ago he had struck his old teacher because he would not answer his question on life and death. Then he repeated the same question to Sekiso. Sekiso said, "I won't say alive, I won't say dead. I won't say. I won't say." At that Zengen came to realization.

Whereupon he left and then shortly returned with a spade on his shoulder and walked from east to west and west to east in the main room of the temple. When Sekiso saw him doing this he said, "What are you doing?" Zengen said, "I am searching for the relics of my old teacher." Sekiso said, "There is a large river with huge waves filling the expanse of the universe. Your teacher's relics are nowhere to be found."

Setcho (Hsueh-tou in Chinese), the compiler of the *Blue Cliff Record*, adds his comment: "Alas, alas." In Engo's (Yuan-wu in Chinese) commentary to the case, another Zen master, Taigen Fu, is recorded as saying, "Aren't your teacher's relics still there?"

Dogo's Chinese name was Tao-wu Wan-chi, and he lived from 769 to 835, in the last of the great T'ang period. He was a dharma heir of Yakusan Igen.

Sekiso, by the way, shouldn't be confused with Sekito, who was a great Zen master and better known than Sekiso. In Japanese he's called Sekiso Soyen, and in Chinese Hsi-chuang Chi-huan. He lived from 986 to 1039 and became a monk in his early twenties. On hearing of Feng-yang Shan-chao, a sixth-generation descendant of the great Rinzai (Lin-chi in Chinese), he went to practice under him. Feng-yang recognized the potential of his new disciple and seems to have devoted special care to his training. For two years Sekiso was denied dokusan, that is, a private encounter with the master. Instead he was consistently driven away with verbal abuse.

How many of us today could stand that? It can take a lot of faith, desperation, and a yearning, truth-seeking mind to continue in the face of whatever the teacher—or life—thrusts our way. Sometimes it seems as if we're always facing obstacles. Yet a real teacher is always trying to help the student face and work through blind spots and shortcomings so that they may awaken. Modern times can make this process much more complex. In the old days most of the serious students were monastics. They lived at the monastery, had made a life commitment to Zen practice, and were ready to take what the master dealt out. Practitioners today are likely to be laypeople and responsible for fulfilling all the normal demands of family life and careers. We have come out of a culture in which Zen and Buddhism can seem new and strange. For most of us, they are not the religion of our parents and extended family. What's more, our culture, our technologies, and our educational system all foster intellectual and mental activities to the degree that self-doubt, mental reservation, anxiety, and skepticism are the norm. People today need some sense of community as well, so the old, direct (and often, by our standards, extreme) methods of the past—except, perhaps, at certain crucial moments— are not likely to be useful.

One night Sekiso came yet again to dokusan. And again, as in the past, he was turned away. He began to complain bitterly, but before he could even finish, Feng-yang sternly scolded him and struck him. Sekiso cried out, but as he did, the master suddenly clapped his hand over his disciple's mouth. With that Sekiso was enlightened.

Sekiso gratefully remained with Feng-yang for years after and eventually received both *inka* (formal acknowledgment that he had completed his training) and dharma transmission from him. He became a noted teacher with several temples under his direction. He died, however, at the relatively young age of fifty-four.

"One day in the neighborhood of Dogo's Temple of Chang-chou, death occurred in a certain home and Zen Master Dogo took his disciple Zengen to express their condolences to the family." In ancient China, monks did not usually hold burial services for people, as is common now. Such services are called *okyo*, meaning literally "reciting the sutras." This kind of service would be performed only when a disciple had died, and so it is likely that the deceased had not just been a student of Dogo's but a lay disciple. During the visit Zengen tapped the coffin and asked, "Is he alive or dead?"

What is Zengen really asking? Obviously he knows that the person in the coffin is dead. So what is his real question? Perhaps it is, What happens after death? or What is death? or What will happen to me after I die? or Is there really death? or If he lies here, dead, what is the Deathless? Perhaps his deep concern—for it is a heartfelt question, as his subsequent actions will prove—grew from, or was intensified by, reciting the *Heart Sutra*: "None are born or die. Nor are they stained or pure, nor do they wax or wane. There is no withering nor death, nor end of them." What does that mean, really? We chant those profound words daily, as do Zen practitioners everywhere. Well, what do they *mean*?

Zengen was deeply troubled by this fundamental problem of life and death. Deep down, aren't we all? Our culture, however, papers this anxiety over with endless distractions: movies, TV, videos, computers, magazines, newspapers, shopping. There are countless potentially addictive distractions available to us. Life's existential anxieties are so very close today, so very clear, perhaps we generate a wall of distractions to keep from feeling constantly insecure. The ancient belief in the harmony of the spheres has given way to one of violent and random catastrophe in deep space. Here on earth we are buffeted daily by reports of the dying of life forms, burning of the rain forests, pollution of the atmosphere and seas; of horrific ethnic cleansings, and the threat of massive political and economic destabilization brought on, in part, by the amazingly rapid evolution of new computer-based technologies. When we open the newspaper, impermanence hits us in the face. Our distractions multiply accordingly, making it hard to keep the real questions, the permanent, gnawing ones that grip our common humanity, in focus: Why was I born? Why must I die? Why is there so much suffering? Still, the questions are really there. Which is why sesshin is such a helpful practice. For a few days, at least, we can be out of the whirlwind and can let our real questions, the ones that persist lifetime after lifetime, generation after generation, arise and be faced head-on.

Zengen had a natural, spontaneously arising, full-time koan. Such a koan, growing out of our own life experience, can be the best koan of all. It raises an existential question and gives us no peace. It is a koan we *must* resolve. Obviously the master knew the depth of Zengen's question, for he wouldn't give in to it, wouldn't placate Zengen with a reassuring answer. He didn't say, Don't worry. It's all right. You'll be reborn according to your thoughts and deeds. Rather, he said, "I won't say alive. I won't say dead." Why not? His disciple was obviously sorely troubled by the whole subject of birth and death, specifically about what happens after one dies.

Once one of the Buddha's monks asked him, "What happens to

the fully enlightened person after death? Does the fully enlightened person exist after death or not?" The Buddha refused to answer. A fully enlightened person is one who has purified his or her mind at even the deepest levels of consciousness, freed it of all the ancient stains of greed, anger, selfishness, and desire. So what happens to such a one after death? Is it the same as for others? The texts say the Buddha "held to a noble silence." There's a very good reason for such a response, as this koan makes clear.

On the way back to the monastery, Zengen is still very bothered. The question keeps gnawing at his mind. He's just seen a stiff corpse. The image is vivid. Where is the owner of the corpse? "Why don't you say?" he demands of his teacher. And Dogo emphatically repeats, "I won't say! I won't say!" Zengen begs, "Please tell me clearly, Master, whether he's dead or alive!" Then, desperate, he cries out in all seriousness, "If you don't tell me, I'll hit you!"

In this we can see just how deeply he feels and what risks he is willing to take to resolve the matter. Hitting one's spiritual teacher is a very serious matter, with profound karmic implications. A student might raise a hand *as though* to strike the teacher, for example, in demonstrating a response to a koan. But for a student to actually hit the teacher is rare and considered quite grave. Yasutani-roshi said that if a monk ever actually slapped the roshi it would have profound repercussions on the whole monastery. But Dogo, unperturbed by Zengen's grave threat, merely answers, "Hit me if you like, but I won't say." Whereupon Zengen hits him.

Time went on. Dogo himself aged and, finally, died. Zengen, still troubled by his unanswered question—and probably also burdened, now that Dogo was dead, by remorse for having struck his teacher—went to see Sekiso, who was by then a well-known Zen master. He confessed to Sekiso how, years earlier, he had hit his old master because he would not answer his question on life and death. Then Zengen again blurted out his buried but still burning challenge: Please give me the answer—I must know! But instead of giving him what he asked for, Sekiso immediately responded, "I won't say alive, I won't say dead." At that, Zengen came to realization.

Just imagine a teacher today who, when asked by a serious student for an explanation about something important, responded, "I'm not going to tell you." It would be seen as an affront to the student and to our whole concept of education. "But you're a teacher!" the student might exclaim. "Your job is to answer questions! Why won't you answer my question?" But Zen masters like Dogo and Sekiso say, You can hit me. You can even kill me. But I won't explain. You must resolve this for yourself. I won't deprive you of your own struggle and your own answer. Long-suffering Job, the biblical patriarch, gets a similar response. All his deep, soul-searing questions are in the end left unresolved by conventional consolations. Only the direct experience of the voice of God speaking from the whirlwind resolves his doubts. That alone answers it all.

Zen students through the ages have expressed deep gratitude to their teachers for having had the wisdom and compassion not to explain too much. This gratitude was not a mere convention, nor was it easily won by any of these men and women of the past. Usually it came after long, hard struggle. Zen master Dogen says, in effect, that Buddhism is nothing more than facing and resolving the problem of birth and death. Zen teaches us how to go beyond ordinary concepts and notions, beyond interpreting the data of the senses to build a worldview of me "in here" and you and everything else "out there." Such a view is incomplete and false. Because it is false and incomplete, we suffer terribly, as fish might suffer swimming in a too-small tank of stale, cloudy water. The masters of many traditions agree that our world, the world we ordinarily live within, is, as the *Diamond Sutra* puts it, like a mirage, a dream, a bubble or foam. That is, it is insubstantial, ever passing, and without abiding reality. This world of birth and death is in constant change. How not to be caught up in it and whirled around by it and, finally, sunk is what Zen practice and training teach us. How to live with constant change and adapt freely to our surroundings, without strain, compulsion, or anxiety, is what Zen practice, Zen training, Zen insight, Zen character are all about. Zen Buddhism is neither pessimistic or negativistic. Rather, it looks squarely at the facts, and then opens a way for us to truly live without continually re-creating suffering.

Still, Buddhism's teachings on rebirth can be confusing in this materialistic culture and time. Buddhism teaches that we have died and been reborn countless times and that we will die and be reborn countless times more. In the writings of the masters we are told that we may be born in any of the six realms: the realms of humans or gods or warring spirits; of hungry ghosts, demonic beings, or animals. We may be born in this realm or that one, in a "higher" or a "lower" form. Sometimes this is interpreted psychologically. My experience in Japan was that the older teachers were less prone to give psychological explanations and tended to believe this in a more deeply mythic way, fully accepting that there are various worlds, dimensions, and realms. The younger teachers were more likely to accept a psychological view. Actually, it doesn't matter whether you approach it psychologically, mythically, physically, or geographically. It all comes to the same thing: in truth, all is constantly changing. And yet within that change there is that which does not change and which makes all change possible. And this is not something that merely takes place after death, after the so-called disappearance of the physical body. At every moment, in every breath, there is life and death. In life there is death, in death there is life. All life is re-creating itself out of its own immolation. All life is a resurrection. How then can we speak of one life and one final death? Dogen says that in life there is only life; in death, only death. So when you're alive you are just one with your whole life; in death you are one with your death. Take a candle burning; the burning is its life as well as its death.

Why, when Zengen comes back after his enlightenment, with a spade on his shoulder, does he walk from east to west and west to east in the main room of the temple? What is the significance of this? Does he want to pay respects to the remains of his teacher, to show gratitude for what Dogo had tried so resolutely to show him? Sekiso sees him marching back and forth and asks, "What are you doing?" Zengen replies, "I am searching for the relics of my old teacher." Perhaps the relics were in that room. Temples often have what we might call a relic room, where memorial tablets are kept. Sometimes the actual bones of a teacher are kept in the temple. Even today there is a short funeral service or chanting of the sutras before the physical body is cremated, after which the bones are usually put into a special container and the ashes scattered. If it's a well-known person, the ashes might be scattered in three or four different places: his or her homestead, perhaps the university where the person taught, and in temples that he or she may have founded. So it's conceivable that the teacher's relics were in the temple.

To return to our question: What was his intent? Sekiso responds, "There is a large river with huge waves filling the expanse of the universe. Your teacher's relics are nowhere to be found." How are we to understand this? There are Buddhist rosary beads, called *juzu* beads, carved in the shape of skulls. The skull represents True Mind, which, like the skull, remains after death. Yet the skull simultaneously represents the reality of death, of universal impermanence. The skull is a very concentrated image, being both a reminder of the so-called relative aspect of death and change and also of what we might call the Absolute, the unborn, the undying.

Is Zengen, by saying that he is searching for the bones or relics of his old teacher—that is, for what remains after death and cremation—suggesting that his teacher's mind is yet to be found? Is he saying that his relics are actually everywhere, in all directions? "Huge waves filling the expanse of the universe" may symbolize our daily lives. Each wave fills the immensity of everything. What is outside it? Being one with your daily life, eating, crying, working, sleeping, loving, each thing done wholeheartedly, singlemindedly, is a vast wave completely filling the universe, reaching to the sky. There's no theory here, no abstraction, no past, present or future, no evaluation. There is just this! What is there to search for?

Setcho's comment is, "Alas, alas!" Taigen Fu comments, "Aren't your teacher's relics still here?"

In demonstrating one's understanding of a koan, one cannot just talk about it. One cannot be theoretical. One has to demonstrate the spirit of the koan, which means, in this case, the spirit of birth and death. This koan, we might say, is only one of a number that deal with the fundamental problem of birth and death, and which demonstrate the existential spirit of Zen teaching.

No matter how much we may try to accept that dying is a simple, ordinary, natural thing, no matter how much we may believe that it is a lofty spiritual experience—a "consummation devoutly to be wished," as Shakespeare so eloquently puts it in the words of Hamlet—we all, if we're honest with ourselves, will also acknowledge that we fear it. It is the undiscovered country, as Hamlet says, from which no traveler returns. It means the end of everything we know, everything we dream of and cling to. As such it can be terrifying. Yet Zen Master Mumon, in the commentary to koan number thirty-five in the *Mumonkan*, titled "Sei and Her Soul Are Separated," says that we go from one minute, one day, one lifetime to the next simply like a traveler changing inns. Or like a flame, which burns up different bundles of wood as it travels along, the flame itself remaining the same. So it is that this energy we call "ourselves" continues to manifest, taking many forms. Then Mumon adds, If we don't really know this—that is, experience it for ourselves—we will, at death, be like a crab thrown into boiling water. It is a horrible image—all those legs writhing helplessly out of control. Mumon concludes: "Don't say I didn't warn you."

Carl Jung, the eminent psychologist, wrote that he never had a patient over forty years of age for whom the real problem was not rooted in the fear of dying—that is, for whom the recognition of the necessity of leaving one's hard-won accomplishments, of leaving life, was not the real obstacle to peace of mind. One can hear many talks about birth and death, and read books about them, but until there is some actual experience of the continuity of life, of what is beyond birth and death and yet not separate from it, there is always bound to be a certain vulnerability. The transformative and liberating power of this experiential truth lies at the heart of this koan.

Of course, the more one hears about the subject of rebirth, the easier it may become for one to accept the idea of such undying continuity. The more one reads about the experience of True Nature, the more some sense of one's real context may sink in. So going to talks and attending lectures and taking time for reading can all be helpful. Reason, after all, tells us that the law of causation is sensible, and that no energy can be lost. Science confirms it. The laws of thermodynamics confirm it. Intellectual reasonableness can grant us some degree of ease until such time as our own experience can confirm it. Still, as useful as such intellectual faith can be, it is limited. It will not stop us from waking in the middle of the night with the awful knowledge that morning only brings us one day closer to the inescapable reality of our own inevitable death.

Zen is the heart of the Buddha's teaching, and as such it deals with the most fundamental problem of all, birth and death, a mystery every human being must resolve. People are not given the choice as to whether this is something they want to deal with. It is our nature, the nature of life, to have to deal with it. It is the teaching of teachings, for it is inescapable. As much as we may wish to avoid the subject, we cannot. Koans are not, as many people think, tricky puzzles. They point us to the realities, the eternal truths, of our ordinary life itself. They reveal fundamental teachings of the Buddha, who was a great realist. He did not invent truths. He experienced and taught what *is*. But koans reveal these truths in a uniquely creative way. Rather than simply describing or talking about them, koans force us to experience these truths for ourselves. And then they prompt us to feel and live from this experience. Rather than adding to our knowledge, they transform us.

There is so much to be grateful for in the simplest mysteries of our ordinary living and dying; so much to be grateful for in our own practice and in these teachings. But if you should ask me, How much? or Why? I could only answer, I won't say. I won't say.

9

Tosotsu's Three Barriers

THE GATELESS BARRIER, CASE 47

Tosotsu made three barriers to test his monks:

"To inquire after the truth, groping your way through the under-brush, is for the purpose of seeing into your nature. At this moment, where is your [True] nature?

"If you realize your own True Nature, you are free from life, free from death. When the light of your eyes is falling, how can you be free from life and death?

"If you have freed yourself from life and death, you know where you will go. When the four elements separate, where are you off to?"

COMMENTARY

If you can rightly give the three turning words here, you will be master wherever you may be and live up to the dharma no matter how varied the circumstances. If, however, you are unable to give them, I warn you, you will get tired of the food you have bolted; well-chewed food keeps hunger away.

VERSE

This one instant, as it is, is an infinite number of kalpas.
An infinite number of kalpas are at the same time this one instant.
If you see into this fact,
The True Self which is seeing has been seen into.

First some background on Tosotsu. Tosotsu Juetsu is the Japanese name for the Chinese Zen Master Tou-shuai Ts'ung-yueh, whose dates are 1044 to 1091. He died at the comparatively young age of forty-eight. He had become a monk at an early age and studied Buddhist philosophy and the Mahayana teachings, and then he got into Zen. One day he visited Master Ungai Shuchi (Yun-kai Shou-chih). Shuchi, aware at once of Tosotsu's learning and of his conceited attachment to it, said to him, "I see you are above the ordinary in character. Why then do you talk and act like a drunk?" Tosotsu got red in the face and sweated at this. His weakness had been penetrated, and he was stuck. But he showed his potential when he finally answered, "I beg you not to deny me your gracious compassion." So Shuchi spoke further with him, probing and pruning him. But the time was not ripe. Tosotsu remained bewildered.

After this, Shuchi allowed Tosotsu to remain and to receive further instruction—that is, to have Zen interviews or dokusan with him. One day Shuchi said to Tosutsu, "Have you been to see Igu of Hosho?" Igu is the name of a master, and Hoshu is the name of a place. Tosotsu replied, "I have seen his *Records* and that was enough. I don't want to see the writer." And then Shuchi said, "How about Tozan?"—another well-known master. Tosotsu retorted, "See that blockhead with his pants stinking of piss? What's he good for?" Shuchi said, "What you must do is make that same stink of piss your own."

Tosotsu acted upon this instruction. He went to Tozan and, under his guidance, at last penetrated deeply into Zen. Then he returned once more to Shuchi, who asked, "How about the Great Thing?" That is, What about enlightenment? And Tosotsu replied, "But for

what you told me to do, I would have wandered in error all my life."
And he thanked him profoundly. After this he began as master at To-
sotsuji Temple, from which he took his name. Here is his death verse:

Two score years and eight
I've got rid of saints and sinners. [Another translation, in
    Shibayama-roshi's *Mumonkan*, has "the ignorant and the
    wise."][1]
Not that I was such a hero.
It's just that the roads of Ryuan were smooth.[2]

Ryuan is a place where Tosotsu lived; "smooth" means that he had
good teachers there.

When Master Shuchi said to Tosotsu, "I see you are above the
ordinary in character. Why is it then that you talk and act like a
drunk?" what did he mean? Tosotsu was very learned, a scholar of
some repute, and it seems he thought this was enough. He thought he
really knew something and was proud of his accomplishment. Shuchi
saw this and revealed it at once. When he asked, "Why do you be-
have like a drunk?" he meant, Why is your mind flopping around so
unsteadily, lost in words, phrases, and concepts? You're not standing
on solid ground at all!

In Tosotsu's response we see his potential. Although caught red-
handed, instead of answering back defensively, he humbly responds,
"I beg you not to deny me your gracious compassion." Realizing the
truth of his own delusion, he sought further guidance. It takes a mature person to respond in this way to an insult. And this is, no doubt,
why Shuchi spoke further with him and had dokusans with him. He
sensed that there was something there, a depth of character, a humil-
ity, a true yearning for Realization that made all the efforts to "probe
and prune" this conceited student worthwhile.

Still, it took time. We see Tosotsu's swaggering ego in his response, "That blockhead with his pants stinking of piss!" He's also
showing a kind of Zen "stink." He's replaced one kind of conceit with
another, perhaps. Or maybe this is his notion of how to respond to a
Zen teacher.

In Zen, although words are used in a very plain way, there's a big difference between testing and challenging a person in order to open a dialogue, and simply being insulting and attacking someone's dignity and integrity. It is very important to make this kind of distinction. Some people seem to think that the dirtier your words, or the ruder you are, the better the Zen you're displaying and the greater the freedom. Actually it may be just the opposite. Everything is in the way you do it, the understanding behind it. Wrongly handled, that is, self-centeredly showing off, you might end up causing harm to someone or getting a well-deserved punch in the nose for your pains.

Now let's turn to the koan. "To inquire after the truth, groping your way through the underbrush, is for the purpose of seeing into your nature." We all begin inquiring after the truth when something has been awakened in us. Perhaps, as in Tosotsu's opening interchange with Shuchi, something gets us to see another perspective. Our old world, our old beliefs and dreams, die, seeming suddenly inadequate or shallow. We may see through them slowly or, as in this case, at once. Perhaps we realize for the first time that we have no grasp of truth. Our pleasures fade, just as they did for Prince Siddhartha, twenty-five hundred years ago, when he awoke to the realities of old age, sickness, and death and set out from his comfortable palace to seek enlightenment. We may think we begin this search because of something from the outside, something we've heard someone say, or someone who has impressed us. But actually this is not so. Something inside us moves. Technically, we can say our karma has matured. And because our karma has matured, something happens. We become open to things that we were never open to before. Suddenly we may find ourselves interested in various teachings. We may begin reading books of one kind or another. We may go to talks. We may become interested in religion, even in the religion of our parents, the one we grew up in. Eventually, through fortunate karmic circumstances, we may meet somebody who really puts us on the path.

Maybe we begin to uncover something that was always there but buried. In the beginning, though, there can be a lot of hesitancy. Unsure of what it is we've found, we may aggressively try to sell our family and friends on it—You ought to try it, it's really great! But we don't convince anybody, really. We don't even convince ourselves, no matter how desperately we try to broadcast our commitment. In the beginning we're always trying to convince ourselves that we're on the right path, because, to be honest, we're still not sure. We have no real grounding in experience. We are still running on dissatisfaction with what has been and hope for what is yet to be. We are still caught between two worlds—one dead, as the saying goes, the other powerless to be born. It's painful, and we desperately try to cover it over with our strenuous assertions. This is why we talk so much.

But then, perhaps, we meet somebody who obviously has "got something." Really, his or her having "something" means that he or she has gotten rid of a lot—a lot of conceit, a lot of self-centeredness, a lot of useless thoughts and useless talk. Having nothing, such a person has everything. He or she is not talking like a drunken person, is not wandering in a dream. His or her feet are solidly on the ground. We don't really know why, but, instinctively, we're impressed. We're impressed not so much because of that person, but because there is that something that has begun to move in us, to awaken, and which now has an initial confirmation: Yes, "it" is true. It can be true.

In my own case, I spent some three years attending the lectures of D. T. Suzuki. I had first met him in Japan, and after talking privately with him for a time and trying to read his books, I began attending his lectures and enrolled in his course on Buddhism at Columbia University. This kind of intellectual approach is almost inevitable as a start. Reason must be satisfied. But it is also possible to get stuck in a rut in which intellectual focus takes the place of actual experience—like Tosotsu at the start.

This "getting stuck" is a kind of misuse of Zen. Instead of taking you beyond concepts, it seems to get you only more and more enmeshed in them. You bolster yourself with them, maybe even make yourself out as sort of superior because of them. It is a sign of desperation, really. You want something to cling to, and you try a conceptual approach to Zen.

Maybe you read a lot about Zen. You hear lectures and talks. You start throwing koans around and tossing new words into your conversations, and it's all very heady and exciting. You kid yourself that you're getting somewhere. In my own case I was lucky at this point to meet a psychiatrist who had had some actual Zen training. Before meeting him, I had imagined that all Zen people simply acted like Dr. Suzuki and that whatever he did, and whatever way he did it, that was Zen. I was amazed to discover that this other person was completely different, a totally different personality from that of Dr. Suzuki, and yet he too was a Zen person. It was a revelation. My karma was ripe, and I was fortunate enough to meet this person— fortunate because it pushed me out of my intellectual rut into finally doing something concrete and tangible. I went back to Japan and began to practice. I got involved with more than just my intellect.

I think the process may unfold like this for many people. Many of us are like the immature Tosotsu at some early point. Yet, if we go on, if we persist, we can also deepen our understanding endlessly.

What, then, is this True Nature we're seeking? It is what enables us to act, to think, to make mistakes; to do wonderful and sometimes terrible things. Whether we're enlightened or not, our True Nature is always functioning. So the mature Tosotsu's question, the question of Tosotsu the enlightened teacher, is appropriate and direct—and uncompromising. At this moment, he asks, Where is your True Nature? Shouldn't we be able to answer this? How can we live not knowing where our True Nature is? If it is our True Nature, where is it? If we ourselves have this True Nature—this undrunken, grounded nature, this awakened nature, this wise and compassionate nature that underlies every act and thought—shouldn't we want to know all about it? Wouldn't we want to know where it is right now?

Suppose somebody said that to you: Where is your True Nature? What would you say? Sometimes people who have read a little Zen will crack the desk with a stick or give a bold shout. Are they really showing where their True Nature is? If you crack a stick and say, Right *here!*—well, then, it can't be over *there*, can it? Our True Nature is everywhere and nowhere at the same time. It has no limitations at all. Saying "here" is itself a kind of limitation. If it's here, then it can't be there. You can't even say it's everywhere, because everywhere has to stand against nowhere. Tosotsu is putting us on the spot by demanding: Tell me right now—where is your True Nature? Show me your True Nature. In the original, it says, "Venerable monk, show me your True Nature." Anyone practicing, anyone searching, really, is worthy, is venerable. Well, if you are worthy, what does your worthiness rest on? Tosotsu is asking us to face this directly. He poses a real test of our life and of our Zen.

Of course, people hearing this may answer, My true nature, as we have just said, is beyond anything. It's in everything. Or it's in nothing. But these are just intellectual statements. These are concepts. We're still a long way from showing our True Nature.

In koan number thirty-seven in the *Mumonkan*, Joshu is asked, "Why did Bodhidharma come from India to China?" Or, in other words, What is the highest principle of Zen? Joshu answers, "The oak tree in the garden."

What is your True Nature? The oak tree in the garden. Is that an acceptable answer? All words are limited in their very nature. Be careful. Be attentive.

Now for Tosotsu's second barrier. By the way, usually we think of a barrier as being a kind of block. But in Zen, a barrier is simply a hurdle to make us jump higher than we normally would. In Zen a barrier is a challenge that gets us to draw on untapped resources lying dormant within us. A famous theme of Chinese and Japanese Zen art is that of a carp leaping up a waterfall. There are many paintings and carvings that show this. In fact, the carp falls back many times. It tries to leap up, over and over. And over and over again it falls back down. At last, drawing on all its will, all its resources and reserves, it makes a desperate, tremendous leap and in an instant reaches the top, the very source of the falls. And there it becomes a dragon. We too must go beyond our ordinary dualistic way of thinking. Tosotsu's barriers will help us.

The second barrier is, "If you realize your own True Nature, you are free from life, free from death." Having passed the first barrier, we come to the second. Realizing our True Nature, we experience our innate freedom. Where is that freedom in our life, in our death? Sometimes it is put, "free from life and death" or even "free from birth and death." Tosotsu challenges us directly. Are you really free?

He knows what it is to talk like a drunken person, and he won't let us off easily. He is pruning and probing us just as Shuchi pruned and probed him. "When the light of your eyes is falling, how can you be free from life and death?" Some people get frightened when they hear this. Why should we be free from life? they think. Death, yes. Who wants to die? But, life? No, not life.

This expression, *life and death*, or *birth and death*, really means change, impermanence, transiency. At every millionth of a second everything is changing. We are being born and dying all the time. Our True Self, our true formless Self, is constantly being transformed according to causes and conditions. To speak of life and death is, in a sense, a kind of anomaly. We should really say life-death. These are two sides of the same thing. Every moment there is life and every moment there is death.

In Buddhism there are two forms of life and death. There is momentary life and death, and there is the life and final death of the physical body. All around us things are born, grow, age, wither, die—and then, if we look carefully, we may also see that they are reborn. Voltaire observed, "It is no more surprising to be born twice than it is to be born once." And yet so many people say, Well, you only live once, so have a good time. But Buddhist and other teachings tell us that we live hundreds and hundreds of times. Even according to science and its laws of thermodynamics and the conservation of energy, no energy can just be lost. It's always transformed. People accept that statement intellectually, and yet, when it comes to one's own body and one's own death, it can be very hard to accept. What? You mean I'll be reborn? You say I've done this before?

Still, no matter how we doubt and resist and fear and suffer and try to run away, acceptance comes, we're told by psychologists who have worked with dying people, even if it's only in the last micromillionth of a second. We accept and die in the end. We have no choice.

But rebirth can be a real stickler. There was a conference in Rochester some years ago on death and dying sponsored by Strong Memorial Hospital and the University of Rochester. One of the participants was a psychiatrist who spoke about what could be done for the dying person. In the question period he was asked, "If the dying person could establish belief, utter faith, in the rebirth process as taught in many religions, wouldn't that help tremendously to make that person's death a calm one? Could that person not more readily and completely accept the fact of death?" He thought a moment and then, astonishingly, said, "No. It has no connection."

There is a great deal of connection. To thoroughly accept the fact of rebirth can make one's whole life altogether different. It can ease attachments, ease fears, assuage guilts and griefs, and give a sense of timelessness to all our efforts to develop and grow. It can give us some sense that moving in the right direction can have meaning, and that we need not judge ourselves too harshly. There will be time, endless time, to complete the work begun in this life.

But the koan says more. It says that you can already be free from birth and death; even in extremis, even as the end of life is upon you, there can be this freedom. "When the light of your eyes is falling, how can you be free from life and death?" How, at the point of death, can you transcend both life and death? There are many kinds of deaths, violent and tragic ones as well as beautiful and calm ones. To die calmly and serenely does not necessarily mean you have transcended life and death. Nor does dying violently in battle, let's say, necessarily mean that you have not. One of the great Zen masters of ancient China, Ganto (his Japanese name), was killed by brigands. He was run through with a sword. As he died, he gave a great shout heard for miles. Centuries later, that shout become a barrier for the young monk who was later to become the great Japanese Zen Master Hakuin. That shout bothered him terribly and gave him no rest. How could a highly developed Zen master die like that, shouting out in death? Where was the transcendence? Once enlightened himself, Hakuin exclaimed that Ganto was unscathed.

There's another story that relates to this freedom in violent death as well. A general in ancient China came to a Zen master. He drew his sword, pointed it at the teacher, and announced, "Don't you know that I am a man who can run you through without blinking an eye?" The Zen master responded instantly, "Don't you know that I am a man who can be run through without blinking an eye?" The general, deeply impressed, sheathed his sword and remained to receive teaching.

Transcending life and death is important not only for the peace of mind that it gives at the time of death, but also for one's rebirth. Buddhism teaches that our mind-state at the moment of death—and here we're talking about the physical death of the body, not moment-by-moment birth and death—determines the quality of our mind-state upon rebirth. Some people think, I'm going to live any kind of life I want to. All I have to do when I'm at the point of dying is to have my mind empty of everything else—or, as Zen Master Bassui puts it, to have a mind as clear as a cloudless sky, not desiring anything. If I do this I'll be reborn in an advanced condition. In that way I can cheat my karma.

Years ago when I was in Burma, I was talking with a Buddhist layman of many years' practice. I brought that question up to him, asking, "Couldn't one cheat one's karma in that way?" He laughed and said, "Unfortunately, it's not that easy. The ordinary person's mind is full of attachments that give rise to fears and and desires. To suddenly find yourself at the point of death and have perfect calmness—not to have even the desire to live again, not to have vain regrets about your life and the way you've lived it, and not to have any fears about what was happening to you—would be impossible. Well, maybe it could happen," he conceded, "if there were the sudden arising of beneficial karma from a past life. But the odds would be entirely against it."

We're told that sometimes a person at the point of death will see a rerun of their whole life. It all passes by in minute detail yet in a flash, as if before their eyes. We may want to do over the things we see, we may want desperately to improve the way we handled certain things, especially relationships. This man had mentioned to me that the desire to be reborn, to repeat the joys and correct the errors of one's life, is one of the most persistent of all desires. Without spiritual training and practice, it is so compelling that it would be almost impossible not be drawn in. To get beyond that, without years of zazen or some other form of meditation, would be like trying to scale

Mount Everest without equipment and with no prior training. As he said, the odds are entirely against it.

Only an awakened mind, or at the very least a disciplined mind, can have this calmness at the point of death. We are taught in Zen that Zen itself is nothing—that is, it is nothing more than being one with every circumstance of your life. If you are at a party, then you are one with being at a party. If you're talking and socializing, then you're talking and socializing. If dancing is going on, you're dancing. Without compulsion or strain you're one with whatever *is*.

Every koan teaches nothing more or less than this total nonseparation. The Truth, the truth of our life, the truth of our True Nature, the truth of the universe, is selflessness, emptiness, Unity. But alas, the minute we say that, we've already implied duality. Unity must stand against plurality. In Zen, to live this truth rather than just talk about it is all. The Truth is not-two. It is not even one. When the light of your eyes is falling, where is your True Nature? Where is your freedom? How will you be free? We are dying all the time.

And so, the third barrier: "If you have freed yourself from life and death you know where you will go. When the four elements separate, where are you off to?" The four elements are, of course, earth, air, fire, and water. In ancient days they were seen as the foundation of all matter. So the question means, when you die and your body decomposes, where will *you* go? Many answers have been given to the eternal question, What happens to me after I die? Yet, as Hamlet says, no one returns from the "undiscovered country" of death to tell the tale. Or do they?

A samurai once asked Zen Master Hakuin where he would go after he died. Since a samurai had to face death almost constantly, it was an appropriate question. Hakuin answered, "How do I know?" "How do you know?" exclaimed the samurai. "You're a Zen master!" And Hakuin said, "But not a dead one." Different Zen masters have given different answers to this question of where one goes after death. Everything really depends on the mind-state of the person who is asking.

We see all around us things being born and things dying. A fundamental teaching of Buddhism is that whatever is born must age and die. Then it will be reborn according to causes and conditions. Our whole life is nothing but cause and effect. Everything that happens, every effect, has an antecedent cause. After we die we will be reborn according to causes and conditions, according to our own thoughts and deeds. People ask, Will I be reborn as a human being or as an ant? You may have the body of a human but the mind of an ant if you've lived like an ant—or like a dog or anything else. In the same human body, there may be many kinds of minds. There can be the highly evolved mind of a compassionate buddha, or there can be the mind of a horseshoe crab. Our life is nothing but karma. The Buddha himself said, in effect, "I don't know what karma is. But I can tell you it works." "It works" means that it is so. It is a fact. On another level, karma means responsibility. One has to take responsibility for all one's actions. You are the architect of your life.

But karma does not mean fate. Fate implies something fixed and unchangeable. In the old Greek sense, fate is something that one struggles against in vain. We say that we have inherited a certain kind of karma, but only certain karmas are fixed—like being born a certain race or nationality, or a certain gender (which at least used to be one of the fixed karmas). But other karmas are modifiable to varying degrees. And there are many kinds of karma. There is individual karma and there is collective karma. There is immediate karma and there is karma that matures at a later time. There is karma from a past life and karma generated in this life. What we're doing in this lifetime creates, hopefully, a more pain-free future karma.

The word karma simply means action and the results of action. All acts and thoughts leave a residue, a pattern. And this pattern conditions our thinking, feeling, and acting. Our karma is always changing according to causes and conditions. Given this, we have the power to change our karma. One way to change it is to do zazen. To sit in meditation is to see into the moment-by-moment flow of causes and conditions. And, while it's true that we have to expiate past karma, the way we expiate it is up to us. Yasutani-roshi used the example of somebody sent to jail for something that he or she had done. How that person spends time in jail will change the karma that put him or her in jail in the first place. Those of you who know anything about

Oscar Wilde's life will see some of this at work. Wilde was witty and brilliant, but also a somewhat frivolous person. And, of course, he was quite an accomplished writer. After he was jailed for homo-sexuality, which was then a crime, there was a complete change in his character. He went through a terrible, soul-searching time and wrote *De Profundis*, a truly profound and deeply personal book, one really worth reading.[3] Cervantes, the old soldier, wrote his great work *Don Quixote* while in prison.

These days, there are people who not only write but do zazen in prison. You are surely changing your karma by making use of your time in that way. Likewise, if you're born with a weak body you can, to a certain degree, and given the time and circumstance, make it healthier. Doctors tend to focus on genetics and inherited traits, but at the same time they would have to admit that we have the power to rebuild ourselves. You can be born sickly, and if you lead a health-ful life, you can become strong. Teddy Roosevelt did that. Con-versely, you can be born healthy, but if you lead a careless life, you will become sick.

The point is that karma should not be confused with fate. Some years ago we had a zazen meeting in Kamakura, while I was training with Yasutani-roshi in Japan. It was on a Sunday. The night before, there had been a horrible head-on collision of two trains, one going from Kamakura to Tokyo and the other one coming from Tokyo back to Kamakura. Two hundred or so people were killed, and many more were injured. It had occurred on a Saturday night at the busiest hour, when the trains were jammed. That Sunday we had our usual zazen meeting in Kamakura. Maybe half a dozen members who were pres-ent had either been on one of those trains or were scheduled to be, but then did not take it for one reason or other. After zazen we had tea with the roshi, and in our conversation the subject of karma natu-rally came up. One person mentioned that for the last six months or so, he had regularly taken that train back to Kamakura, but on the night of the crash, something had come up and he didn't take it. He said that he had had a very fortunate karma. The discussion then turned to the matter of responsibility and karma. Of course the karma of the train engineers was mentioned, and that of those who had been injured.

Then Yasutani-roshi said the most surprising thing: "All those who were on that train were at least fifty percent responsible for the accident." Everybody threw up their hands in exasperation and surprise. "Impossible!" people exclaimed. "It was the engineers who were responsible! Why hadn't they been alert and aware of the signals? That is their job!" And indeed, as it turned out, one engineer had been drinking, and the other had been laid up after having been out late at a party. There was also the possibility that the flagman hadn't given the right signals. It was a mess.

But Roshi insisted. "Spiritually speaking," he said, "those who chose to be on that train have half the responsibility for what occurred. No one was forcibly put on that train. Had they been, they would have borne no karmic responsibility. At least they would not have been karmically culpable."

His comment caused quite a stir. So we see that karmic culpability and legal liability are two very different things. Just imagine saying to your lawyer as he prepares to sue the railroad company on your behalf, "Wait. Don't sue. I'm fifty percent responsible. I'm guilty of contributory negligence." Well, if you were lucky, perhaps your lawyer might think your mind had been affected by the accident and make a claim for you on that basis.

"When the four elements separate, where are you off to?" That is, where will you go? We all know that the light of our eyes must fall. We all know that the four elements must separate. All right, where will you go? Where do you go? To really know that, to be able to demonstrate that in dokusan and in life, is surely worth working hard for. Zen is not easy, but it offers a lot. And it offers nothing at all.

Mumon's commentary on the koan is: "If you can rightly give the three turning words here, you'll be the master wherever you may be." What are these turning words, one for each barrier? In case number fourteen of the *Mumonkan*, "Nansen Cuts the Cat in Two," Master Nansen finds the monks arguing about a cat. Perhaps they were arguing about whether or not it had buddha-nature. He demands a word of Zen from them and threatens that if none is offered, he will kill the cat. The monks are stunned and cannot respond. Alas, poor cat! (Most masters agree that Nansen would not actually kill the cat. He probably mimed it vividly, though.) When Joshu returns to the monastery and hears of the monks' argument and his teacher's challenge, he takes off a sandal, puts it on his head, and walks out. Nansen approves of his "word of Zen," saying, "If you had only been here, you would have saved the cat." A word in Zen does not necessarily mean syllables. It means a true response.

If you can give these turning words, Mumon says, "you will be master wherever you may be." What does it mean to be such an absolute master? Most of us are slaves to the circumstances of our lives, that is, slaves to our thoughts. We like to think of ourselves as being free, and we tend to imagine our freedom in economic or political terms. How many people think of freedom in terms of freedom from the weight of their own conditioned thinking? Of course, we should distinguish between thinking something through creatively and just being driven by thoughts. The random irrelevant thoughts that are constantly going through our minds and taking our minds captive are not the same as the focused intention of meaningfully directed thought.

To be master of your life means to know where you are at each moment—not to be pulled this way or that, not to be unconsciously driven; it means having the freedom to move one way or the other, to do something or not do it, without any regret or compulsion. It also means not to be completely torn down by unfavorable or painful circumstances and not to be ecstatically, euphorically elevated by favorable ones. It means being free of attachments, free of the addictive need to grasp at people, things, or even concepts.

"Turning words" are words that open the mind, words that turn the mind from bondage to freedom and from delusion to insight. If you can rightly give the turning words, you can "live up to the dharma no matter how varied the circumstances." What is the dharma? The dharma is no more nor less than the law of cause and effect. This is the Buddhist teaching that everything at every moment is changing and a new self is constantly being created. There is no enduring permanent self. To live life in this way is freedom. When you're eating, you just eat and then you're through. When you're working, you just work and then you're through. It's not such an easy thing to do. We carry around lots of thoughts, especially about our work. We can get so taken up with work. We have to learn to take one thing at a time, to be fully one with it and then, when it's over, to be fully one with whatever's next.

But if you are unable to give these turning words, Mumon cautions, "you will get tired of the food you have bolted; well-chewed food keeps hunger away." There are various interpretations of this warning. Some people understand it to refer to a shallow enlightenment or to training that is superficial or incomplete. A shallow kensho is not fully satisfying. One has seen into constant change, it is true, and into the formless Self as well—that which makes change possible. One has caught a glimpse of both change and changelessness. But it's only a glimpse, and it is not enough, because, in reality, the two worlds of change and changelessness are not really two at all. After a time this initial seeing makes us want to go further, deeper. Instinctively we know that it's only well-chewed food that nourishes and satisfies. This we might take as meaning long training through which we more fully integrate our understanding into our daily lives. Our enlightenment is fully digested. Now change is Changelessness. This is what keeps away hunger, uncertainty, anxiety, fear, and above all unsatisfactoriness, the constant feeling of being on edge, alienated, separated—"a stranger and afraid," as the poet A. E. Housman wrote, "in a world I never made." At last we know real peace.

The verse says: "This one instant, as it is, is an infinite number of kalpas." What is a kalpa? The sutras describe a kalpa as the length of time it would take a heavenly being, or deva, sweeping its gossamer wings across the top of a mile-high mountain once each year to wear that mountain down to the ground. This one instant is a kalpa. All time is in this instant, and an infinite number of kalpas are, at the same time, this one instant. All time means past, present, and future. These are themselves arbitrary notions, an arbitrary slicing up of time. What do we mean by time? Shakespeare says time must have a stop. We can stop time if we stop thinking in terms of time. How do we do that? Do we think in terms of timelessness? We just fall into another hole if we do. "I must stop thinking in terms of time" is still "I" opposed to "time." It remains dualistic. But, if our mind is entirely free from both time and timelessness, if we are living fully and wholly every moment, every moment is everything; all of time is in each full, vitally alive moment.

If one has truly seen into time and timelessness—if one has really become time itself—then there is no notion of time or timelessness to hinder or bind. As long as we're obsessively thinking of and planning for the future, the always-vague, indefinite future, and as long as we're mulling over, regretting, replaying the past, we've separated ourselves from life and death and are trapped by it, cut off from our real, living present. Of course, if one wants to go to college, let's say, or get married, one has to make certain plans and prepare for what is to come. But so many people are tormented by the future, obsessively laying up money and possessions, constantly bartering their present and banking on a future that may never come. This is the tragedy of it. The future is in the past, and the past is in the present. And the present is beyond future, past, and even present. If you see into this, the True Self that is seeing has been seen into.

So long as we are separated from things, so long as we think of ourselves as a subject, "I," confronting people, things, ideas, we have not seen into our True Self. When we see into the True Self, there is no True Self. A monk once came to a Zen master and said, "I've come here to train myself in order to solve the question of life and death." The master drove him away saying, "Here there's no such thing as life and death." This is true. The whole notion of life and death is self-created. As long as we are separated from life, we think about life and death. The person who is fully one with his or her life cannot think about it because that person does not step back from it, does not make it an object to consider. In a well-known enlightenment story cited in *Three Pillars of Zen*, a Japanese executive writes of his experience:

The big clock chimes—not the clock but the Mind chimes. The universe itself chimes. There is neither Mind nor universe. Dong, dong, dong!

I've totally disappeared. Buddha is!

"Transcending the law of cause and effect, controlled by the law of cause and effect"—such thoughts have gone from my mind.[4]

Seeing into the True Self, one does not think "cause and effect," or "subject to or not subject to life and death." All such concepts arise from a dualistic relationship to life. Mumon says, "The True Self which is seeing has been seen into." It is seen into the instant one leaps these fine hurdles that Tosotsu so compassionately puts before us.

10

Kicking Over the Pitcher

THE GATELESS BARRIER, CASE 40

When Master Isan was training under Hyakujo, he worked as tenzo at the monastery. Hyakujo wanted to choose an abbot for Daie Monastery, so he summoned the head monk and the rest of the disciples to make their Zen presentation, and said that the ablest would be sent to found the monastery. Then he took a pitcher, placed it on the floor, and said, "Don't call this a pitcher but tell me what it is." The head monk said, "It can't be called a wooden sandal." Hyakujo then asked Isan his opinion. Isan walked up, kicked over the pitcher, and walked away. Hyakujo laughed and said, "The head monk has lost." Isan was ordered to start the monastery.

COMMENTARY

Extremely valiant though he was, Isan could not jump out of Hyakujo's trap. Upon careful examination, we see he followed what is heavy, refusing what is light. Why? Taking the towel band from his head, he put on an iron yoke.

VERSE

> Throwing away the bamboo baskets and wooden ladles,
> Isan with a direct blow cuts off complications.
> The barrier Hyakujo set up for Isan did not stop him.
> The tip of his foot creates innumerable buddhas.

Hyakujo and Isan were two great Chinese Zen masters at the end of the T'ang period. There are many anecdotes about Hyakujo, which is his Japanese name. He is Pai-chang Huai-hai in Chinese.

One day Isan was with Hyakujo, who suddenly asked, "Who are you?" Isan replied, "Fayu," his ordinary, given name. (As with most Zen monks, he took his Zen name from the mountain, in this case Mount Isan, where the temple was situated.) Hyakujo said, "Just rake the fireplace and see if there are any live coals." Isan raked it a bit, then said, "There aren't any." Hyakujo got up and, raking down deep, brought up a burning ember. He lifted it, exclaiming, "Is this not fire?" At that, Isan's darkness lifted, and he was enlightened.

Do you see the connection between asking him "Who are you?" and the ember? Notice that Hyakujo brings up a small burning ember, maybe even a tiny one. "Is not this fire?" he exclaims. People sometimes feel that they are inferior, or lack this or that. They think, Oh, I've got such a strong ego and such heavy karma that I could never come to awakening. In one contemporary enlightenment story, a monk, now a roshi, by way of encouragement says, "Even in the driest hole one can sometimes find water."[1] No one need feel that he or she hasn't the capability. Buddha-nature is already present. You don't have to get or add anything. In a live, burning fashion Hyakujo brings this point home to Isan: Here it is!

Hyakujo is famous in Zen for many accomplishments. Besides being an outstanding teacher, it is said that he also established the first monastic rules in Zen. He insisted that monks take vows and also—this was a major change from the wayfaring life of Indian Buddhists—that they must work, that is, do actual physical labor in the fields. He felt strongly that monasteries and monastics should be self-supporting.

Another of his rules was that monks should not eat outside the regular meal times. His rules were intended to help keep the community of practitioners functioning smoothly, so as to create the least possible impediment to the realization of their goal of a life of awakening. The most original feature of Hyakujo's monastic system lies in his insistence on the obligation of work—which extended even to the abbot himself. Before this time monks were not supposed to engage in any physical labor, which was left for laypeople. This is still essentially the practice in India and Southeast Asia.

In the traditional Indian practice, monks went out begging alms and remained dependent on the supporters of the monastery or the temple to sustain them. The idea was that being free of the requirements of menial work, they could more actively engage in their studies and formal practice, and in this way most quickly become of benefit to the community. Of course, the climate of India and Southeast Asia helps make such a lifestyle possible. Another reason that monks were forbidden to till the ground was a literal upholding of the precepts; hoeing and plowing would inevitably lead to the killing of worms, snakes, mice, and insects. Such killing, it was felt, even though inadvertent, would generate negative karma. Given this, monks were expected to abstain from such work and the possibility of transgressions.

But to the practical-minded Chinese, living in a much colder, drier climate, these notions did not sit well. Why should able-bodied monks live like parasites on the sweat and labor of others? This issue has been a theme throughout Chinese Buddhist history. At times it led to the destruction of monasteries and the forced return to lay life of many monastics by imperial order. For this and other reasons, Hyakujo wisely required his monks to work tilling the fields and producing crops so that they could live on their own labor and only secondarily on the donations and alms of the lay community.

There were profounder reasons, of course, than economic or political ones for this change. Physical work actually makes it easier to do mental work. It's easy to become sluggish and torpid when one is sitting and studying all day. Today many people whose work is mental, such as office workers, exercise at gyms for exactly this reason—to counter the negative effects of a sedentary life. Zen traditionally incorporates all this and does so in a spiritually significant context. One Japanese practice, *takuhatsu*, going out for alms, is an example of how the physical and spiritual can be united. *Takuhatsu* involves walking, often for many miles in all kinds of weather. Holding up an offering bowl while begging and chanting sutras may be physically demanding, but through it the teachings are shared in a direct way with believers, who, in turn, offer food to the monks. Thus everyone feels connected. This builds mutual respect and keeps a community of belief alive. A respect for the energizing effects of physical work, for the ordinary, common life, and for the abilities of our own marvelous bodies are fundamental to Zen. All this we owe to Hyakujo.

Still, some feel that manual work is beneath them. It's not "cultured." How sad this is. To work physically is to rediscover one's body and to empower it. One feels alive while working physically. One's muscles move, one breathes deeply, one sweats and wipes one's brow. The mind clears and comes to a focus on the task at hand. Also, one is more obviously contributing something useful to the community: preparing food that nourishes, bringing wood for the fire, creating a clean zendo to sit in, building a sturdy shed to store tools. Looked at this way, physical work is anything but demeaning.

Hyakujo's most famous and revolutionary dictum was, "A day of no work is a day of no eating." He also insisted that the monastery should be subject to the assessment of taxes for its crop yield on an equal basis with laypeople. He was criticized by conservative elements in the Buddhist community for this, but he stood his ground. He was politically astute and spiritually democratic. Yet what he was introducing seemed very radical at the time.

Interestingly, these very changes that Hyakujo so conscientiously and independently made have all become key elements of the Zen we know today. What a remarkable, strong-minded person Hyakujo was! Those who think that egolessness means a weak personality should think again. Hyakujo lived till the ripe old age of ninety-four and insisted on working almost up to the day he died. By the way, he also insisted that to become a *shramana*, or novice, at his monastery, applicants had to take the five precepts: not to kill, not to steal, not to have improper sexual relations—which, in the case of a monastic, of course, would be any sexual relations—not to lie, and not to take intoxicating liquors or drugs that confuse the mind.

In 840, when Buddhism suffered its worst persecution in the history of China, the sect that survived best was Zen. This was because the Zen monks remained independent through working and raising their own food. They lived very simply in the mountains, cultivating the fields and themselves in remote, relatively inaccessible places. They did not accumulate riches, possess many ornate, gilded Buddhas, or try to establish lavish temples. The late T'ang era saw the worst persecution, yet there's hardly any mention of it in the koans and stories. Homage to Hyakujo!

Once a monk asked Hyakujo, "Who is the Buddha?" The master responded, "Who are *you*?" Such a simple reply, yet one that goes to the heart of the matter: Where are you looking for Buddha? Who or what do you think Buddha is? Hyakujo tosses the question right back at the questioner, "Who are *you*?" He was practical in every way. Homage, indeed.

Isan (Kuei-shan Ling-yu) lived from 771 to 853 and was a noted monk. In time he was to found a Zen line of his own. Of course, masters don't really "found" sects or lines in the sense of setting out to do so. Rather, followers seem to gather around some masters over time, and then pass on the teachings they receive, which then further evolve in their own ways. Thus a new line of Zen is "founded."

Isan seems to have been a mellow, quiet person of modest temperament. He wasn't one who disported himself in remarkable or dramatic ways. A monk once asked him, "What is the Tao?" He replied, "Mindlessness is the Tao." The monk said, "I don't comprehend." Isan said, "All you need do is to apprehend the one who does not comprehend." The monk came back again, saying, "Who is the one who does not comprehend?" Isan answered, "He is none other than yourself."

Once Isan said to his monks,

I wish to see all persons now living know how to experience directly their selfhood. Know that the one who does not comprehend is precisely your own mind, precisely your buddha. If you gain bits of knowledge and information from the outside, mistaking them for Zen or Tao, you are quite off the mark. This kind of learning is like dumping dross upon your mind rather than purging it of dross. Therefore I say it is not the Tao at all.[2]

Lao-tzu, the great Chinese sage, said, "The practice of Tao consists in daily losing." This is perfect Zen, which evolved in China when Indian Buddhism and Chinese Taoism met. Not surprisingly, Zen retains many elements of its Taoist heritage.

Another aspect of Isan's teaching is its insistence on instantaneous enlightenment rather than so-called gradual cultivation. There seems to have been some confusion during this period about teachers upholding a path of gradual enlightenment. In fact, there's no such thing as gradual enlightenment, but there is gradual cultivation. Once a monk asked Isan, "After a man has attained instantaneous enlightenment, must he still cultivate his spiritual life?" This is a question many wonder about, if not ask. Many people imagine that with enlightenment, especially full enlightenment, there's nothing more to do because you're finished, graduated, perfect. Not so. You've only graduated from one school to go on to the next. As Dogen says, there is no end to practice.

Isan's response to this crucial question is clear and direct:

If a man is truly enlightened and has realized the fundamental, and he is aware of it himself, in such a case he is actually no longer tied to the poles of cultivation and non-cultivation. But ordinarily, even though the original mind has been awakened by an intervening cause, so that the man is instantaneously enlightened in his reason and spirit, there still remains the inertia of habit, formed since the beginning of time, which cannot be totally eliminated at a stroke. He must be taught to cut off completely the stream of his habitual ideas and views caused by the still operative karmas. This (process of purification) is cultivation.[3]

In Zen it's said that after enlightenment it is absolutely essential to continue training. Of course, training after enlightenment is different from training before. Here is how Isan describes it:

> I don't say that he must follow a hard-and-fast method. He need only be taught the general direction that cultivation must take. What you hear must first be accepted by your reason; and when your rational understanding is deepened and subtilized in an ineffable way, your mind will of its own spontaneity become comprehensive and bright, never to relapse into the state of doubt and delusion.[4]

Let us be clear about this: "What you hear must first be accepted by your reason." He's not simply saying that to attain the deepest truth you must go beyond the reasoning mind. It's said that an elephant will not step on a plank or a log unless it first tests to be sure that it will bear its weight. The elephant is cautious, and rightly so, given its great bulk. In the same way, the rational mind often must be assured that one is going in the right direction, that one is secure, before it can give itself completely to any particular direction in life or toward any meaningful plan, spiritual or otherwise. If it is not sure, if there are too many unexamined reservations, these can become lodged in the subconscious, where they remain and can—and often do—become a barrier. Later they can even become a kind of hazard, all because the mind wasn't truly convinced at an earlier stage. In other words, if the needs of reason are not given their proper and appropriate due, if one tries to ignore the promptings of one's own intelligence, then at a later stage suppressed reservations will come up to plague the mind. In Zen this means that one's practice drifts, and one cannot move along until these very doubts—quite different from the "doubt mass" of deep questioning that fuels the quest for awakening and liberation—are at last resolved. Still, it is also true that "the heart has its reasons that reason will never understand." Balance is all.

"Never to relapse into the state of doubt and delusion." This doubt really means skepticism: "However numerous and various the

subtle teachings are, you know intuitively how to apply them—
which to hold in abeyance and which to develop—in accordance
with the occasion."[5] This may seem difficult for many people. How
do you know, they ask, what is the right thing to do in such-and-
such a situation? How do you know that you are doing the right
thing? Through training in Zen, particularly when it includes koans
with their focus on responsiveness—grasping a situation whole and
bringing it immediately to life—you come to know how to respond
freely, wholeheartedly, spontaneously. You don't know how you
know, but you know. You simply find that you can, when you've
trained yourself this way, respond in accordance with what the situation calls for, without any reference to whether it is "right" or
"wrong."

Isan continues:

> To sum up: It is of primary importance to know that Ultimate
> Reality or the Bedrock of Reason does not admit of a single speck
> of dust, while in innumerable doors and paths of action, not a sin-
> gle law or thing is to be abandoned. And if you can break through
> with a single stroke of the sword, without more ado, then all the
> discriminations between the worldly and the saintly are annihi-
> lated once for all, and your whole being will reveal the truly eter-
> nal in which reigns the nonduality [of universal mind].[6]

There is a story about a disciple of Isan's named Yang Shan. When
Yang Shan entered the dokusan room, Master Isan said, "Say something immediately. Do not enter shadowy realms." Yang Shan at once
replied, "I do not even formulate my creed." The master probed further. "Do you believe in a creed which you refuse to formulate, or is
it that you really believe in no creed and therefore you have nothing
to formulate?" Yang Shan clarified the point. "Whom else can I believe than the inner Self?" "In that case you are a *shravaka* of a set
mind," rejoined Isan. A *shravaka* is a follower of the Buddha. But the
disciple responded, "I see no Buddha." Isan took that up at once,
pressing further. "In the forty rolls of the *Mahaparinirvana-sutra*, how
many words are the Buddha's and how many the demons'?" Yang

Shan immediately answered, "All words belong to the demons." The master was delighted. "Hereafter," he exclaimed, "no one will be able to get the better of you."

People get attached to the concept of God, even to the concept of Buddha. Joshu in his old age is reported to have said, "If there's one word I don't like to hear, it's the word *Buddha*." For some of us today, the one word we don't like to hear is *God*. It's thrown around all the time, shamelessly so, God this and God that. People speak as if they know what God wants, what God demands, what God thinks, what God blesses, what He curses and damns—even what wars God supposedly wants us to fight and what sinners and what sins God wants us to condemn. We take such liberties with the mystery of God. Indeed, much evil has been done in the name of God—"for God's sake," with God's supposed blessing. Poor God! He or She deserves our deepest pity.

To return to the beginning of the koan: "When Master Isan was training under Hyakujo, he worked as tenzo in the monastery. Hyakujo wanted to choose an abbot for Daie Monastery, so he summoned the head monk and the rest of the disciples to make their Zen presentation, and said that the ablest would be sent to found the monastery." *Tenzo*, by the way, means the one in charge of food. Hyakujo, as the teacher, had a good idea of the qualities and abilities of his different disciples, and for reasons best known to himself, he didn't feel that the head monk was right for the abbot's job. He wanted Isan to go. Perhaps he knew that Isan was the most advanced of the monks, or simply the most suited for this particular task.

And so he arranges this revealing little drama. Taking a pitcher, he places it on the floor and demands, "Don't call this a pitcher but tell me what it is." The head monk says, "It can't be called a wooden sandal." This is not a bad answer. The name is purely an arbitrary designation, isn't it? Still, if you just call it a not-pitcher, you're negating the fact. So what do you do? Then Hyakujo calls on Isan. Isan walks up, kicks over the pitcher, and leaves. Hyakujo laughs, saying, "The head monk has lost." And he orders Isan to start the monastery.

What is so good about Isan's response? What is the significance of what he did? In this we see the free-working of Zen at its best. Both

Hyakujo and Isan move the play along. What was Isan expressing? Suppose he had picked up the pitcher and gone through the motions of drinking from it. Would that have been acceptable? Suppose he'd taken the pitcher and thrown it away or dashed it to the ground, smashing it to pieces. Would that have been a good response?

There is a difference between "live" Zen and what could be more properly termed a display of ego. Those who may have studied a little Zen or read many anecdotes, perhaps some like this one, may imagine that to do whatever you feel like doing is good Zen. These persons may then imitate the masters, not really understanding what's involved. This is not freedom but confusion.

The difference between authentic Zen and mere imitation is the extent to which the ego is involved. But even that's not always so obvious. Some might even think that in this particular koan there's egotism because of the seeming competitiveness. But accomplished Zen people enjoy this "dharma dueling." It's a testing of spiritual muscles, just as with young people who may spar and wrestle with each other. There's a vitality and a joy in it. And through the process of dialogue and challenge and counterchallenge, truth is revealed. There's no "Zen stink" to this whatsoever. But playing to the gallery and showing off is something very different.

Zen activity, functioning freely and unimpeded, without constraint or inner bondage, is not random or capricious. It may look like that, but it's not. There is a natural flow and spontaneity, with an almost inevitable quality to it, even though you may not see that inevitable aspect at first. It arises intuitively, and those who are intuitively sensitive can see beneath the action a strength and centeredness, a kind of lightness and aplomb that defies logic. Like a lid that perfectly fits its box, the action fits the situation with nothing lacking and nothing in excess. And then it's over, just as when Isan kicks over the pitcher. If he had picked it up and hurled it, or if he had smashed it, it wouldn't have been the same at all. We may call it a pitcher, but it is much more.

A Japanese Zen master once said to his monks, "Imagine that the pitcher was Mount Fuji. It's easy enough to kick over a pitcher, but how would you kick over Mount Fuji? And if you couldn't kick it over, what would you do?" What would *you* do? To properly grasp and respond to this koan, one has to grasp the live mind of Isan and bring it forth.

Mumon comments, "Extremely valiant though he was, Isan could not jump out of Hyakujo's trap." Was it a trap? If so, in what respect? "Upon careful examination, we see he"—meaning Isan—"followed what is heavy, refusing what is light. Why?" Isan could have gotten out of the heavy burden of taking on the job of starting up a new monastery—in the wilderness, no less! He could have easily "failed" the test if he'd been "smart" enough to see through it. Then he could have remained where he was, doing the less formidable work of running the kitchen as compared to starting a monastery. Why didn't he maneuver to get out of it? He knew the burdens involved.

Sometimes it is hard for people to comprehend the power of the selfless mind that emerges in practice. It's as if we have uncovered an ancient power, and we want, above all else, to use it to help all sentient beings. Nothing else will satisfy. Opening up a temple is certainly an expression of that. So while Isan could have remained where he was, working hard in the kitchen—actually one of the most demanding of all monastery jobs—his compassion was too primed by now for him to be satisfied any longer by that. It was simply impossible for him to sidestep the challenges of the project before him. In fact, to have shrunk from it would have been more difficult than plunging into it. One simply must do what one is called to do. And there's also the fact that his teacher asked him to do it. Of course Hyakujo knew that Isan was the right person for this daunting assignment! Isan and Hyakujo were a perfect match, teacher and disciple seeing eye to eye.

"Taking the towel band from his head, he put on an iron yoke." The towel band is what Japanese monks wear today as they work. Evidently this was customary in ancient China too. Mumon is saying that he took off the towel band appropriate to strenuous kitchen work and put on an iron yoke, shouldering the great responsibility of opening a temple and teaching.

Mumon's verse:

Throwing away the bamboo baskets and wooden ladles,
Isan with a direct blow cuts off complications.
The barrier Hyakujo set up for Isan did not stop him.
The tip of his foot creates innumerable buddhas.

The bamboo baskets and the wooden ladles, of course, are the accou-
trements of the kitchen. "Isan with a direct blow cuts off complications"—what do you suppose "complications" here refers to? Is it all
kinds of talk about a thing we call a pitcher? To say a thing is this
or a thing is that—doesn't this create complications? All manner of
difficulties spring from this dividing of the world, this limiting and
confining the truth of different things, this binding and chaining of
each thing.

We are dealing with what we conventionally call a pitcher, but
we could just as well call it Mu. We reduce the reality by arbitrarily
calling a certain object "a pitcher." A pitcher has to be shaped a certain way and used in such-and-such a manner. And a pitcher is made
out of metal or porcelain, and a pitcher is this size or that size, and
has a handle, and so on. Before we know it, we're far removed from
the reality itself. Through these notions, these arbitrary conceptual-
izations that we make about things, we are constantly creating complications and barriers. And we're caught in them.

We do the same thing with time. We slice time into past, present, and future, forgetting in the process that time in its fundamental
sense is unsliceable. It's convenient for us to do this and allows us to
manipulate time. It's actually too convenient, for unless we retain an
awareness of timelessness, we soon find ourselves caught, dragged forward and pulled backward by times to come and times past. We
have put another yoke on our own shoulders, created another barrier
to our own free flow. The present is gone. Trying to set up timelessness as the solution cannot solve it either. Another yoke. How do you
kick over and show the whole pitcher?

Zen does not have a quarrel with words as such. One doesn't become free by *not* calling it a pitcher, by avoiding words. Zen is a
teaching outside the sutras, beyond words and letters. It cannot be

contained by words and letters, for it is not possessed or bound by them. Rather, when one is beyond words and letters, one can use them freely, wisely, spontaneously. What does it mean to be beyond words and letters? Is Zen in pitchers and towels? Does it disappear in words? Zen expresses itself in live words, those which issue from the gut, those which emerge from the deepest emotions and fire the imagination; such words are very much admired and used in Zen. They are Zen.

> The barrier Hyakujo set up for Isan did not stop him.
> The tip of his foot creates innumerable buddhas.

A synonym for *buddha* is *freedom*, the freedom to move in any direction in accordance with conditions. Not being tied to a concept or a no-tion—or a particular gesture—is to be a buddha. "The tip of his foot creates innumerable buddhas." Such a one can come and go, can kick the thing, can kick it up high in the air, can kick it over, can smash it to bits, can pick it up and drink from it. Glug glug glug! He or she is not constricted by self-consciousness or, indeed, by any notion at all. There is no need to say or know what a thing should or should not be, or what he or she should or should not do. Such a person does not have to prove a thing.

As we said earlier, only through long training can a truly natural spontaneity manifest itself. It takes many years of practice. As long as one is self-consciously standing apart from other people or things, there can't be free-flowing movement. Ideas of oneself or of things are always in the way. In free-flowing action, everything is embraced and nothing excluded. A great deal of energy, joy, and élan come out of living this way, not only for the person who actually attains such flow, but for everyone. This Way has a terrific power to stimulate in the best sense, to inspire and awaken.

Certainly innumerable buddhas spring from the tip of Isan's foot. With a single kick a pitcher tumbles, water spills out, a monastery appears high in the mountains, and new buddhas, training there, spring forth. How could it be otherwise?

Kempo's One Way

THE GATELESS BARRIER, CASE 48

A monk once asked Kempo, "The Bhagavats of the ten directions have one road to Nirvana. Where, may I ask, is that road?" Kempo held up his stick, drew a line [in the air], and said, "Here."

Later the monk asked Ummon's help. Ummon held up his fan and said, "This fan has jumped up to the thirty-third heaven and hit the nose of the deity there. The Dragon-Carp of the Eastern Sea makes one leap and it rains cats and dogs."

COMMENTARY

One goes to the bottom of the deep sea and raises a cloud of sand and dust. The other goes to the top of the towering mountain and raises foaming waves that touch the sky. The one holds, the other lets go, and each, using only one hand, sustains the teaching of Zen. What they do is exactly like two children who come running from opposite directions and crash into each other. In this world such people who grasp truth directly are difficult to find. But if we look at these two great teachers with a true eye, neither of them really knows where the Nirvana road is.

VERSE

Without raising a foot we are there already;
The tongue has not moved, but the teaching is finished.
Though each move is ahead of the next,
Know there is still another way up.

Not much is known about Zen Master Kempo except that he was a successor to Tungshan, who was considered to be the founder of the Soto sect. He seems from the evidence of this koan to have been forthright and direct.

We do know a great deal about Ummon (Yun-men in Chinese), one of the great figures in Chinese Zen. There were said to be five central houses, or lineages, of Zen during the glorious T'ang period. One of these was the house of Ummon. In *The Golden Age of Zen*, John Wu writes:

> Ch'an masters, like other men, may be divided into two types: some are slow breathers, others are fast breathers. Of the founders of the five houses of Ch'an, Kwei-shan, Tung-shan, and Fay-en belong to the slow breathers, while Lin-chi and Yun-men belong to the fast breathers. Of these two, Lin-chi breathes fast enough, but Ummon breathes faster still. Lin-chi's way is like the Blitzkrieg. He kills his foes in the heat of battle. He utters shouts under fire. When the lion roars, all other animals take cover. No one can encounter him without his head being chopped off by him. It makes no difference whether you are a buddha, a bodhisattva, or a patriarch, Lin-chi will not spare you if he should by chance encounter you. So long as you bear a title or occupy any position, Lin-chi will send out his True Man of No Title to kill you off in a split second. So terrible is Lin-chi. But more terrible is Yun-men.
>
> Lin-chi only kills those whom he happens to encounter. Yun-men's massacre is universal. He does away with all people even before they are born. To him, the "True Man of No Title" is al-

ready the second moon, therefore a phantom not worth the trouble of killing. Yun-men seldom if ever resorts to shouts or beatings. Like a sorcerer he kills by cursing. His tongue is inconceivably venomous, and, what makes the case worse, he is the most eloquent of the Ch'an [Zen] Masters.[1]

Once Ummon recounted the legend of the Buddha's birth, of how the baby Buddha, with one hand pointing to the heavens and the other to the earth, took seven steps and declared, "Above the heavens and below the heavens, I alone am the Honored One." Then Ummon added, "If I had been a witness of this scene I would have knocked him to death with a single stroke and given his flesh to dogs for food. This would have been some contribution to the peace and harmony of the world."[2]

It seems as though Ummon was not in awe of anyone. He once quoted the famous dictum of the great Confucius: "He who hears the Tao in the morning can die in the evening." Then, without even mentioning the name of the revered sage, he commented, "If even a worldly man could have felt like that, how much more must we monks feel about the one thing necessary to us."[3] All was simply meal for grinding in Ummon's dharma mill.

Here's another of Ummon's sayings: "Even if I could utter a wise word by the hearing of which you would attain an immediate enlightenment, it would still be like throwing ordure on your heads." And another time he said, "Do not say that I am deceiving you today by means of words. The fact is that I am put under the necessity of speaking before you and thereby sowing seeds of confusion in your minds. If a true seer should see what I am doing, what a laughing-stock I would be in his eyes. But now there is no escape from it."[4]

Ummon lived from 864 to 949 and seems to have been unusually eloquent as a child. Precisely because he was so adroit and adept at using words, he truly understood their danger. In the koans, the mondo, and the sayings of the masters we continually find this deep understanding of language. Clearly words and language are one of the wonders of the human mind. Yet the masters nonetheless caution us to be alert lest we become ensnared and entangled in them. The veil of words, it has been said, can all too easily cover over direct experience like a glove. Lost in words, we wander far from our real lives.

In working with students, Ummon was famous for his one-liners, that is, for his ability to respond immediately with penetratingly direct verbal thrusts. In this he seems to have been something of a genius. "The moment you step into my door," he said, "I already know what kind of ideas you have brought with you. What's the use of again raising the dust long settled in an old track?" People today, too, sometimes come into dokusan (the private interview with the teacher) and begin digging up emotions and feelings. We are so ready to go over the same old stuff and raise the dust of the same old track. We have been shut up within our own thoughts and memories for so long, we sometimes hardly seem to know what to do with freedom. By clinging to and then juggling old trinkets of thought and emotion, we trap ourselves. Carrying the corpse of dead emotions and disinterring buried feelings, we bury the present, the future, and even the past. It may seem natural enough, but it is really a deadening and deadly way to live.

People often want to understand the meaning of recurring thoughts, emotions, and images. To answer plainly: they have no particular meaning, at least not in an ultimate sense. On a psychological level they do have meaning, and it can be quite helpful to air them, to acknowledge and work with them. But Zen does not engage directly in the psychological realm. This is why psychotherapists can be helpful to Zen students. When D. T. Suzuki gave a series of lectures to psychiatrists in New York City, he drew one of the largest audiences he ever had. It's not hard to understand why psychotherapists would be interested in Zen. Zen deals with the mind; the mind is the basis of Zen and of psychotherapy. But the two deal with the mind, with Mind itself, in different ways. Both can be valuable.

To continue with Ummon, here are several more of his penetrating "no-gap" responses.[5]

"What is the right Dharma Eye?"

Answer: "All-comprehensive."

"How do you look at the wonderful coincidence between the chick tapping inside its shell and the hen's pecking from the outside?"

Answer: "Echo."

"What is the one road of Ummon?"

Answer: "Personal experience."

"What is Tao?"

Answer: "Go."

"Our late teacher remained silent when the question was put to him, 'What shall we enter as your epitaph?' "

Answer: "Teacher."

"One who is guilty of patricide can repent and vow to amend his life before Buddha, but if he has killed the Buddha and the patriarchs, before whom can he repent and make the promise to amend?"

Answer: "Exposed."

In Zen it's said—Rinzai being the source—"Kill the Buddha! Kill the patriarchs!" That is, should the Buddha or dharma ancestors arise as images in your mind, cut right through them. Don't be subservient! Don't cling to the past! Experience what they experienced for yourself. Then let them go! So the monk's question had an edge: "If you've accomplished the Buddha Way and stand alone in the universe, to whom do you turn then?"

Let's return now to the case of the koan. "A monk once asked Kempo, 'The Bhagavats of the ten directions have one road to Nirvana. Where, may I ask, is that road?' Kempo held up his stick, drew a line [in the air], and said, 'Here.' "

"Bhagavats of the ten directions have one road to Nirvana" is a quotation from the *Surangama-sutra*. *Bhagavat* is a Sanskrit term referring to one of lofty spiritual attainment. It refers here to a buddha. The ten directions mean north, south, east, west, nadir, zenith, and the intermediate directions. In other words, it means everywhere. As I mentioned in my first talk, the word *nirvana* is one of those words that has come in for a lot of abuse. Many early Western writers on Buddhism were missionaries, and what they understood and wrote about Buddhism was filtered through their own set of cultural and religious assumptions. They took the word *nirvana* at its literal meaning of "extinction," and then seized upon the implication that Buddhism must be a terribly negative religion. To them *nirvana* came to mean the extinction of the individual. Since they assumed that each individual possessed an immortal soul, such extinction must have seemed like the spiritual equivalent of a lobotomy.

Yet if we compare the central images of Christianity and Buddhism, we find on the one hand a person hanging in agony, suspended irrevocably between heaven and earth; and on the other a person sitting calmly touching the earth, an archaic smile on his lips. Which seems more negative, life-denying, frightening? Of course, we should not take Christianity at face value and miss the deeper symbolism of Christ's immense anguish. Still, one can only wonder what Asian Buddhists first thought of Christianity.

In Mahayana Buddhism, *nirvana* actually means eternal or absolute; it implies calm joy and the extinction of all suffering. So while nirvana does literally mean "extinguished," in the sense of a flame being blown out, the extinction to which it refers isn't that of the individual but of all illusory, limiting, pain-causing concepts, images, and notions. Nirvana really means awakening to a supremely liberated state of being. It literally means the blowing out of the fires of suffering.

Entering nirvana carries the implication of leaving the physical body behind, thus suggesting death. This also helps explain the negative connotations that have surrounded the word. People habitually think that life is wonderful and death horrible, as though there were a clear separation between them. But the Buddhist experience is that ultimately there is no separation between them at all. Life and death form one seamless whole. They are really "life-and-death." From the Buddhist perspective, things just as they are, imperfect as they are, are the Absolute, are the Unbounded, are nirvana. *Samsara*, the world of birth and death, *is* nirvana.

How can this be? We know from our own lives that things change and die, and that this unrelenting impermanence can be terribly painful. When the monk asks, Where is the one road to nirvana? he is voicing our own question, the question we ask every day. Why is there pain and suffering? Why is there loss and anguish? Why the Holocaust and nuclear weapons and poverty and ethnic cleansing and environmental pollution? Why death and change? How, given this, do I find peace and happiness? Tell me, where is the one road to nirvana?

In the opening lines of his *Divine Comedy*, Dante says that in the middle of his life's journey he awoke to find himself alone, lost in a dark wood, having strayed from the true path. We each at some point awaken to find ourselves alone in a dark wood, our easy answers gone, the path unclear, the journey confusing. And we begin to really want to know how to get onto the one road. The question, Where is the one road? is an eternal and universal question that can be found at the heart of all religions and all human lives.

For Buddhism and Hinduism there are not only innumerable worlds, as modern astrophysics is now making clear—worlds beyond worlds beyond worlds—but also innumerable states of consciousness. Worlds without and worlds within. Endless worlds. Some of these states include bodies, some are bodiless conditions of pure consciousness. In this koan we get to face the eternal question of the One Road, but we also get to soar beyond the vast reaches of the thirty-three heavens.

The Buddha's passing from life is described in Buddhist teachings as a "parinirvana." That is, it was not death as such, but an entrance into complete nirvana, in which the limitations of a conditioned body and mind are completely transcended. Then truth, wisdom, awareness, energy, bliss, and selfless, compassionate activity are unimpeded. Final nirvana is actually a dynamic and vital state, not a static condition of nothingness or rest.

The sutras also tell us that, in truth, this condition alone is real. Yet it is exactly what we, in our ordinary condition, find so hard to believe. You mean there's a state of absolute bliss, wisdom, and compassion, and that alone *is*? And that is actually my true nature?

Yet the word *nirvana* is hardly ever used in Zen. It seems so remote, so "in the future," so terribly far from our present moment and present activities. While training in Japan, I don't think I ever heard the word *nirvana* used except in a commentary on a koan such as the one we're discussing here. In terms of the day-to-day activities of normal training, even in teishos (the formal Zen talks by the roshi), it just wasn't used. Even when I was in a monastery in Burma I seldom, if ever, heard the term *nirvana*. Yet it's actually a rich word with powerful and inspiring connotations.

Our monk has heard in the sutras about the one road to nirvana, and now he wants to know where it is. Without an instant's pause, Kempo raises his stick and draws a line in the air—"Here." A horizontal line is the figure 1 in Chinese characters. The one road to nirvana, where is it? "Here." Is there any place where the one road isn't? We stand up, we sit down, we eat, we wash up. We're happy and we laugh. We're sad and we cry. We burn our finger and cry "Ouch!" We step outside our door and say "Good morning" to our neighbor. The truth is before us. The road is under our feet. We walk the road asking, Where is the road?

Perhaps this monk was troubled. Perhaps he thought, There is a road, a way to peace and freedom. All the bhagavats know it. Well, then, where is it? I don't see it! If that was his mind-state—and perhaps it was and perhaps it wasn't; he might have known the road well and been challenging Kempo, you'll have to decide—but if it was, perhaps Kempo's clear and direct response intensified that doubt.

The monk next goes to Ummon for help. He asks his troubling question; Ummon holds up a fan and says, "This fan has jumped up to the thirty-third heaven and hit the nose of the deity there." Ouch! "The Dragon-Carp of the Eastern Sea makes one leap and it rains cats and dogs." It pours and pours and pours, cats and dogs. Swish! Swish! Swish! There goes the dragon carp! Ummon was never one to sit quietly. He too demonstrates the dynamic and unfathomable one road.

As I mentioned in discussing "Tosotsu's Three Barriers" (chapter 9), in Zen the carp leaping upstream is used as a symbol of the Herculean effort we must make to attain awakening. Like the carp, we must leap beyond the endlessly rushing waterfall of our habitual thoughts, judgments, and desires. We give our all and fall short, again and again. Then at last, in desperation, we make a final, all-out effort and go beyond ourselves. Reaching the Source, instantly the most ordinary carp becomes a dragon!

Sometimes paintings of the carp show the lovely figure of Kuan-yin standing on its back, directing it through the seas of life. Kuan-yin, or Kannon in Japanese, symbolizes compassion. What moves the carp to become a dragon is compassion. At bottom, this is what fuels our effort and mobilizes our courage, fortitude, and determination. While this effort may at a certain point take the form of desperation, it is really compassion that motivates the leap. We see the sorrows of the world, we experience our own sorrows, and we must *do* something. To actualize our innate compassion and make real our innate desire to help others—to reach this state and attain full enlightenment—takes effort. It involves sacrifice, which implies making something sacred, not just giving up or losing something. It demands that we endure some discomfort. To attain anything of real worth, we must make difficult choices and be willing to bear hardship. In the verse to case number seventeen in the *Mumonkan*, "The National Teacher Calls Three Times," Zen Master Mumon says, "If you want to support the gate and sustain the house, you must climb a mountain of swords with bare feet." In other words, to attain true understanding requires a sustained and deeply committed exertion. The exertions of a woman in childbirth are often long and prodigious too, yet babies are born every day. If you want to know about it, ask a mother.

Or, if it's enlightenment you want to know about, ask Ummon. He is not just talking about it, he's demonstrating it. When there is no sense of a limiting self, one acts directly and fully from one's essential Mind. The impossible becomes possible, and the smallest act is a miracle that evokes gratitude and delight. This freedom is the dragon's true condition. But as long as there is a thought in the mind of wanting to do this or to achieve that, there is limitation. Then one falls back and is again a carp looking up at the towering waterfall. One of the masters said, "What one understands is only half-true. What one doesn't understand is full truth." As the commentary to case number nine in the *Mumonkan* puts it, "When the ordinary person realizes, he is a sage. A sage if he understands is an ordinary man." Real nonunderstanding is not so easy to come by. One must ascend a mountain of swords with bare feet and leap to the top of a mountain-high waterfall.

The commentary to the present case by Zen Master Mumon goes like this:

> One goes to the bottom of the deep sea and raises a cloud of sand and dust, the other goes to the top of the towering mountain and raises foaming waves that touch the sky. The one holds, the other lets go, and each, using only one hand, sustains the teaching of Zen. What they do is exactly like two children who come running from opposite directions and crash into each other. In this world such people who grasp truth directly are difficult to find. But if we look at these two great teachers with a true eye [of the absolute point of view], neither of them really knows where the nirvana road is.

The expressions "holding" and "letting go" refer to the two "sides" of Reality, which really has countless sides—and no sides at all. The one side is the world of the ten thousand things, to use a Zen expression—that is, the limitless range of forms. And the other side might be called no-thingness, or emptiness. "Vast emptiness and nothing to be called holy" is how Bodhidharma put it. Letting go is releasing all things, letting them be as they are, and affirming the phenomenal world. Holding fast to the world of the Absolute is seeing through the phenomenal world. It is negating or denying, for it is speaking from the "other side," the side of "no-thingness," where there is "not a single blade of grass." It is empty of all concepts, all separately conceived "things."

Koan number fourteen in the *Mumonkan*, "Nansen Cuts the Cat in Two"—like all koans, really—highlights first one side of Reality, then the other. In the first half of the koan, Nansen cuts the cat in two. (Remember, he mimed it. No Zen master would actually kill a cat to demonstrate Buddhist teachings.) This is holding fast, killing, or negating the world of distinct phenomena. In the second half Joshu puts a slipper on his head and walks out, affirming or letting-be the phenomenal world once again, returning to the world of the senses. Presenting this side, the master is "giving life" or "releasing" or "unrolling." It also relates to the discipline of ongoing spiritual practice and to the ordinary activity of our consciousness in the world of form. This is where we have cause and effect, right and wrong, and so on.

Although we speak of these two worlds as though they were two, in reality they are not. They are not even one! "Form is only empti-ness, emptiness only form," affirms the *Heart of Perfect Wisdom* or *Prajna-paramita-sutra*, which Zen students in training centers chant daily. Kensho is grasping this directly and intimately. To see emptiness clearly is really to see form. They are inseparable. To cling to form and fail to see emptiness is to fail in the end to truly see form itself.

"One goes to the bottom of the deep sea and raises a cloud of sand and dust." Does the bottom of the deep sea relate to the emptiness aspect and the sand and dust to the phenomenal? Yet how can it be that at the very bottom of the ocean there is dust?

That towering mountain in the other half of this image, does it signify emptiness, while the foaming waves are the limitless comings and goings of the world of form? But how can there be waves at the top of a mountain? It makes no sense. Yet it is absolutely true.

Each of these teachers, in his own uniquely personal way, is fully expressing both worlds. Actually, we can't even say "both worlds," because there are really not two worlds at all. So for convenience's sake, we might say "two *aspects* of reality." We might say "form-and-emptiness-as-not-two."

When we talk as I am talking now, it is dry, because it is explana-tory, and the imagination is not touched at all. But if you say, "One goes to the bottom of the deep sea and raises a cloud of sand and dust, the other goes to the top of a towering mountain and raises foaming waves that touch the sky," the imagination is stirred to life. We are engaged, alert. It catches our attention. It's like looking at a Chagall painting in which embracing couples fly through the air. It seems like a topsy-turvy world. It seems impossible. But it is also a clear expression of the world of Reality beyond logic and reason. Again, if you say "the world beyond logic and reason," it sounds so dry and philosophical. How much better to say, "The one holds and the other lets go, and each, using only one hand, sustains the teaching of Zen. What they do is exactly like two children who come running from opposite directions and crash into each other." *Wham!*

"If we look at these two great teachers with the true eye, neither really knows where the Nirvana road is." After praising them, Mumon seems to be putting them down. Mumon loves to praise by slander. Does anybody know where the road to nirvana is? What do you think? Can anybody say anything about it? Could even the Buddha—the great expert on nirvana—really tell us a thing? Understanding is not the point. When a sage understands, the sage becomes common. There's no line, no arrow pointing out this one road. In our True Mind we can't speak of knowing or not-knowing. In koan number nineteen in the *Mumonkan*, Joshu, while still a young man, asks his teacher, Nansen, "What is the Way?" Nansen replies, "Your everyday mind is the Way." Joshu asks, "How do we get onto it?" Nansen responds, "If you try to direct yourself toward it, it goes away from you." "But if we don't try to direct ourselves to it," Joshu persists, "how will we know it is the Way?" Nansen answers, "The Way does not belong to knowing or not knowing. Knowing is an illusion and not-knowing is blankness. If you attain to it, you'll see that it's as limitless as the vastness of space."

> Without raising a foot, we are there already;
> The tongue has not moved, but the teaching is finished.
> Though each move is ahead of the next,
> Know there is still another way up.

There's no place to go and no place to return to. Why, then, do we rush around so? In our daily lives we're constantly striving to accomplish this and achieve that. Many people are trying to help others and do good in a very positive sense. Yet Lao-tzu says, "It is more important to be good than to do good." If you are good, then everything you do will be good. If our True Nature is everywhere, in an Absolute sense, how can we even move? What is there to move? And where is there to move to? Only something bound by time and space can move from "here" to "there." So many people feel so small, so powerless. To catch even the smallest glimpse of this marvelous, nothing-lacking buddha-mind gives us a new sense of our unlimited potential. All the wonder and mystery of creation is in each one of us. We need only open ourselves up to see it.

"The tongue has not moved, but the teaching is finished." All wisdom, all virtue, all goodness is already within each of us. It is our birthright. Why, then, do we act so often like fools—or worse? This is the sad predicament of humanity. Our discriminating minds supposedly place us "above" the other animals. But they also create many problems. Adam and Eve ate the apple from the Tree of the Knowledge of Good and Evil and knew for the first time that they were naked. With this bifurcating knowledge of good and evil, we have created so much pain and have done terrible things. Even religions, which came into being to help us live well, have been fighting one another for millennia. Somebody once said to me, "Since there are so many religions already at odds with one another, why add another by becoming a Zen Buddhist?" For me Buddhism is not a religion in the sense of Christianity, Judaism, or Islam. Harada-roshi used to say, "If you're constantly talking about Buddhism, it's not Buddhism you're talking about." And there is, of course, no God-concept in Buddhism. To some this may sound as heretical as Voltaire's statement to the effect that opinion has caused more suffering than all the world's epidemics. In the same way, the *notion* of God has caused more suffering than any other concept that has lodged in the human mind. This does not mean that there is no transcendent reality. But in Zen Buddhism what is vital is to *experience* it, not reduce it to words, concepts, and symbols.

Though each move is ahead of the next,
Know that there is still another way up.

In the ancient game of *go*, a sort of cross between checkers and chess, each move is the foundation for the next. So too in life: we make our moves, earning degrees, getting married, adding on to the house, paying off the mortgage. In our practice we work hard, go to sesshins, perhaps have a kensho. It's only a beginning. How far can we go? When you've done everything, tried every route, there is still another way up. Although one step follows another in neat progression, there is still another way. You don't have to wait until the last number has been set in place, the last note played, or the final i dotted. There is another way up, always there, beyond sequence and logic. Because this is so, you can *leap*. Or you can simply let go of the cliff. The road to nirvana, where is it?

"Here!" proclaims Kempo.

Where, would you say, is that?

Notes

The cases from the *Mumonkan* and *Hekiganroku* quoted in this book are taken from working texts for students at the Rochester Zen Center and its affiliates, as compiled and adapted by Roshi Philip Kapleau from his notebooks and from translations of the *Mumonkan* by R. H. Blyth and by Zenkei Shibayama; and from translations of the *Hekiganroku* by Thomas and J. C. Cleary and by Katsuki Sekida.

INTRODUCTION

1. Zimmer, *Philosophies of India*, 544.
2. Shibayama, *Zen Comments on the Mumonkan*, 100–01.

CHAPTER 1: THE BUDDHA HOLDS UP A FLOWER

1. Adapted from a Japanese poem, author unknown.
2. Shibayama, *Zen Comments on the Mumonkan*, 63.
3. Ibid.
4. Ibid.
5. Ibid., 61.
6. Ibid., 62.
7. Ibid., 65.

CHAPTER 2: A WOMAN COMES OUT OF MEDITATION

1. Shibayama, *Zen Comments on the Mumonkan*, 296.
2. Ibid.
3. de Bary, *Buddhist Tradition*, 363.

CHAPTER 3: A NON-BUDDHIST QUESTIONS THE BUDDHA

1. From *The Buddhacharita* by Ashvaghosha, as quoted in Conze, *Buddhist Scriptures*, 62.
2. Shibayama, *Zen Comments on the Mumonkan*, 231.
3. Hakuin, *Song in Praise of Zazen*, a version created for chanting at the Rochester Zen Center and its affiliates.
4. Shibayama, *Zen Comments on the Mumonkan*, 232.

CHAPTER 4: VIMALAKIRTI'S GATE OF NONDUALITY

1. Kapleau, *Three Pillars of Zen*, 343.
2. This account of the events preceding the koan is taken, with numerous adaptations, from Robinson, *Vimalakirti Sutra*, 18.

CHAPTER 5: BODHISATTVA FU LECTURES ON THE *Diamond Sutra*

1. Miura and Sasaki, *Zen Dust*, 262–4.
2. Diamond Sutra, 61.

CHAPTER 6: LAYMAN P'ANG'S BEAUTIFUL SNOWFLAKES

1. Miura and Sasaki, *Zen Dust*, 303–5.
2. Ibid., 304.
3. Ibid., 305.

4. Sasaki, Iriya, and Fraser, *Man of Zen*, 18–26, 39–43.
5. Wallace Stevens, "The Snow Man," in *Collected Poems of Wallace Stevens* (New York: Knopf, 1969).

CHAPTER 7: GOSO'S NO WORDS OR SILENCE

1. Adapted from Blyth, *Mumonkan*, 242.
2. Shibayama, *Zen Comments on the Mumonkan*, 256.

CHAPTER 9: TOSOTSU'S THREE BARRIERS

1. Shibayama, *Zen Comments on the Mumonkan*, 317.
2. Blyth, *Mumonkan*, 302.
3. Oscar Wilde, "De Profundis," in *The Portable Oscar Wilde*, ed. Richard Aldington and Stanley Weintraub (New York: Penguin Books, 1946).
4. Kapleau, *Three Pillars of Zen*, 231.

CHAPTER 10: KICKING OVER THE PITCHER

1. Kapleau, *Three Pillars of Zen*, 254.
2. Wu, *Golden Age of Zen*, 160.
3. Ibid., 162–3.
4. Ibid., 163.
5. Ibid.
6. Ibid.

CHAPTER 11: KEMPO'S ONE WAY

1. Wu, *Golden Age of Zen*, 212–3.
2. Ibid., 213.
3. Ibid.
4. Ibid., 214.
5. Ibid., 220–1.

Glossary

Abbreviations: *Ch.: Chinese; Jap.: Japanese; Skt.: Sanskrit.*

ANANDA: the Buddha's disciple and attendant, also his cousin, known for generosity and refinement of character—and for his phenomenal memory. With it he retained and transmitted to others all the Buddha's DHARMA discourses. He became the Third Patriarch of Zen in India, receiving transmission from the First Patriarch, Mahakashyapa.

AVATAMSAKA-SUTRA (Skt.; Jap., *Kegonroku*): a profound MAHAYANA sutra embodying the sermons given by the Buddha immediately following his perfect enlightenment.

BIRTH AND DEATH: see SAMSARA.

BODHIDHARMA: the Twenty-eighth Patriarch in line from the Buddha, the First Patriarch of Zen in China. Scholars disagree as to when Bodhidharma came to China from India, how long he stayed there, and when he died, but it is generally accepted by Japanese Zen Buddhists that he came by boat from India to southern China about the year 520 and that after a short, abortive attempt to establish his teachings there, he went to Lo-yang in northern China and finally settled in Shaolin Temple, located on Mount Su. Here for nine years he steadily did ZAZEN. This period has come to be known as his "nine years of facing the wall."

BODHI-MIND: intrinsic wisdom; the inherently enlightened heart-mind; also the aspiration toward perfect enlightenment.

BODHISATTVA (Skt.): an enlightened being who, deferring his own full buddhahood, dedicates himself to helping others attain liberation. In his self-mastery, wisdom, and compassion a bodhisattva represents a high stage of buddhahood, but he is not yet a supremely enlightened, fully perfected buddha.

BODHISATTVA VOWS: see FOUR VOWS.

CH'AN (Ch.): Zen; from Sanskrit *dhyana*, meditation.

CONSCIOUSNESS ONLY SCHOOL (Ch., *Wei-shih*; Jap., *Yuishiki*; Skt., *Vijnanamatra*): doctrine of the eight kinds or levels of consciousness, ranging from the senses (including mental cognition), through an abiding sense of individual or ego consciousness, to the storehouse consciousness, or *alaya-vijnana*.

DEVA (Skt.): literally, "one who shines." A heavenly being analogous to (but not identical with) an angel in Western spiritual cosmologies. The deva realms are said to be characterized by great happiness and ease and are the highest of the six realms of unenlightened existence. Like all karmically conditioned states or realms, they are temporary. See also KARMA.

DHARMA (Skt.; Jap., *ho*): a fundamental Buddhist term having several meanings, the broadest of which is phenomenon. All phenomena are subject to the law of causation, and this fundamental truth comprises the core of the Buddha's teaching. Thus dharma also means law; ultimate truth; the Buddha's teaching; and the doctrines of Buddhism.

DHARMA ANCESTOR: one of the men or women of the past who attained full enlightenment and who taught the DHARMA.

DIAMOND SUTRA (Skt., *Vajracchedika Prajnaparamita-sutra*; Jap., *Kongokyo*): one of the most profound of the MAHAYANA sutras. It concludes with the words, "This sacred exposition shall be known as the *Vajracchedika* [diamond cutter] *Prajnaparamita-sutra* because it is hard and sharp like a diamond, cutting off all arbitrary conceptions and leading to the other shore of Enlightenment."

DOKUSAN: private encounter with a Zen teacher for the purpose of clarifying one's understanding of the DHARMA.

FOUR VOWS or BODHISATTVA VOWS (Jap., *shiku seigan*): vows as old as MAHAYANA Buddhism. In the Zen temple they are recited three times in succession after the close of ZAZEN: "All beings without number I vow to liberate. Endless blind passions I vow to uproot. Dharma gates [that is, levels of truth] beyond measure I vow to penetrate. The Great Way of Buddha I vow to attain." In the *Platform Sutra of the Sixth Patriarch*, Dharma Ancestor Hui-neng gives these vows a profound interpretation.

GATELESS BARRIER: see MUMONKAN.

HEKIGANROKU (Ch., *Pi-yen lu*): *Blue Cliff* or *Blue Rock Record*. Probably the most famous Zen book, it consists of 100 koans compiled by Zen Master Hsueh-tou Ch'ung-hsien (Ch.; Jap., Setcho Juken; 980–1052), with his own commentary in verse accompanying each KOAN. Every koan is preceded by an introduction containing the gist of the koan, by Zen Master Yuan-wu (Ch.; Jap., Bukka Engo; 1063–1135). The book derived its name from a scroll containing the Chinese characters for "blue" and "rock," which happened to be hanging in the temple where the collection was compiled, and which the compiler decided to use as a title for his work.

HUI-NENG (Ch.; Jap., Eno; 638–713): the Sixth Patriarch (DHARMA ANCESTOR) of Zen in China counting from BODHIDHARMA, the Twenty-Eighth Indian Patriarch and the First Chinese Patriarch. The record of Hui-Neng's life and DHARMA talks can be found in the *Platform Sutra of the Sixth Patriarch*. Said to have been illiterate, he had a first awakening when, as a young man selling firewood, he happened to hear a monk chanting a verse from the DIAMOND SUTRA.

JOSHU JUSHIN (Jap.; Ch., Chao-chou Ts'ung-shen; 778–897): a renowned master of the T'ANG period. His Mu is the best known of all KOANS. Joshu is said to have attained KENSHO at the age of eighteen and complete awakening at fifty-four. From fifty-four to eighty he made pilgrimages around China, staying with prominent masters and engaging in "dharma dueling" with them. Not until he was eighty did he formally open a monastery and begin to teach. He then continued to instruct students until his death at the age of 120. Like his master, Nansen, Joshu was mild-mannered. He eschewed the vigorous speech and violent actions of RINZAI, yet his wisdom and acumen in dealing with students was such that he could convey more with gentle sarcasm or a tilt of the eyebrow than other masters could with a shout or a crack of the stick. This is clear from the numerous koans that revolve around him. Joshu is highly admired in Japan.

KARMA (Skt.): one of the fundamental doctrines of Buddhism. Karma is action and reaction, the continuing process of cause and effect. Thus our present life and circumstances are the products of our past thoughts and actions, and in the same way our deeds in this life will fashion our future mode of existence. The word *karma* is also used in the sense of evil bent of mind resulting from past wrongful actions.

KASHYAPA: Mahakashyapa, one of the Buddha's great disciples and the First Buddhist Patriarch. He received transmission of the DHARMA directly from the Buddha. Also known as Kasho.

KENSHO (Jap.): literally, "seeing into one's own nature." Semantically, *kensho* and SATORI have virtually the same meaning and are often used interchangeably. In describing the enlightenment of the Buddha and the great masters, however, it is customary to use the word *satori* rather than *kensho*, *satori* implying a deeper experience. (The exact Japanese expression for full enlightenment is *daigo tettei*.) When the word *godo* (literally, "the way of enlightenment") is combined with *kensho*, the latter word becomes more subjective and emphatic.

KOAN (Jap.): in the original Chinese, a case that establishes a legal precedent. In Zen, a koan is a formulation, in baffling language, pointing to ultimate truth. Koans cannot be solved by recourse to logical reasoning but only by awakening a deeper level of the mind beyond the discursive intellect. Koans are constructed from the questions of disciples of old together with the responses of their masters, from portions of the masters' sermons or discourses, from lines of the SUTRAS, and from other teachings. The word or phrase into which the koan resolves itself when grappled with as a spiritual exercise is called in Japanese the *wato* (Ch., *hua t'ou*). Thus, "Has a dog the Buddha-nature?" together with Joshu's answer, "Mu!" constitutes the koan; "Mu!" itself is the *wato*. Altogether there are said to be 1,700 koans. Of these, Japanese Zen masters use a core of about 500, since many are repetitive and others less valuable for practice. Masters have their own preferences, but invariably they employ (if they employ koans at all) the MUMONKAN and HEKIGANROKU compilations of koans. A disciple who completes his or her training under Yasutani-roshi must pass the following number of koans and other types of problems in this order: miscellaneous koans, 50; *Mumonkan* (with verses), 96; *Hekiganroku*, 100; *Shoyoroku*, 100; *Denkoroku* (with verses), 110; *Jujukinkai* and others, 90—a total of 546.

KYOSAKU (Jap.): "encouragement stick" used during rounds of ZAZEN to refresh and encourage sitters. Usually a wooden stick, two to three feet long, flattened at one end, it has been used in Zen training for centuries as an aid to concentration. Each shoulder is struck once or twice on points corresponding to acupuncture meridians to rouse slumbering energies, especially during long stretches of sitting.

LAO-TZU: Although Lao-tzu is commonly regarded as one of China's greatest sages, little is known about his actual life. He is said to have been born about 604 BCE, and to be the author of the *Tao-te Ching* (*The Way and Its Power*), which is the bible of Taoism, as the religion which grew up around this book came to be called. The Tao has been defined as the ground of all existence, or as the power of the universe.

LIN-CHI I-HSUAN: see RINZAI GIGEN.

MAHAYANA (Skt.): "Greater Vehicle," one of the two main branches of Buddhism. Also known as the Northern School, Mahayana Buddhism spread from northern India to Tibet, Mongolia, China, Vietnam, Korea, and Japan. The Mahayana emphasizes the compassionate ideal of the BODHISATTVA—one who strives for enlightenment not simply for the welfare of the individual self, but for the liberation of all sentient beings. Zen is a central form of Mahayana Buddhism.

MAITREYA (Skt.; Jap., Miroku): the "Great Loving One," the BODHISATTVA who will become the Buddha of the next world cycle. Presently in the Tushita Heavens, Maitreya is developing the skillful means (UPAYA) to liberate suffering beings.

MAKYO (Jap.): various illusory experiences, visions, and sensations that can arise as the surface levels of the mind settle during extended periods of ZAZEN. Ultimately anything less than enlightenment is a *makyo*. There are many kinds and levels.

MANJUSRI: see SAMANTABHADRA AND MANJUSRI.

MONDO (Jap.) literally, "question and answer," a uniquely Zen type of dialogue, often between a master and a student, wherein the student asks a question on Buddhism that has deeply perplexed him or her, and the master, skirting theory and logic, replies in such a way as to evoke an answer from the deeper levels of the student's intuitive mind.

MUMONKAN (Jap.; Ch., *Wu-men-kuan*): *The Gateless Barrier*. This book of forty-eight koans, with comments in prose and verse by the compiler, Zen master Wu-men Hui-kai (Jap., Mumon Ekai), is the best-known collection of Chinese koans next to the HEKIGANROKU. The verse accompanying each koan is usually treated as a separate koan.

NIRVANA (Skt.): extinction of ignorance and craving and awakening to inner peace and freedom; nirvana stands against SAMSARA, that is, birth and death, or the world of relativity. Nirvana is also used in the sense of a return to the original purity of the Buddha-nature after the dissolu-

tion of the physical body, that is, to the perfect freedom of the unconditioned state.

NOBLE TRUTHS: said to have been the subject of the Buddha's first
DHARMA talk after his great enlightenment. They are: (1) the universal-
ity of suffering, (2) the causes of suffering, (3) the cessation of suffering,
and (4) the path leading to the cessation of suffering—the Noble or
Eightfold Path.

P'ANG YUN: (Ch.; Jap., Ho-koji; c. 740-?): Layman P'ang, a great T'ANG
dynasty Zen figure and man of means who, it is recorded, dumped his
entire fortune of gold into a river and thereafter wandered about the
country with his family, earning his living as a maker of bamboo ware
and engaging in "dharma dueling" (MONDO) with famous Zen masters.

PARINIRVANA (Skt.): literally, "complete extinction." This term most frequently refers to the passing away of the Buddha.

PRAJNAPARAMITA-SUTRA: the *Heart Sutra*. The heart (*hridaya*) of the vast
Prajnaparamita (wisdom) literature, this SUTRA is recited so frequently in
the temple that most Zen students chant it from memory. Its theme is:
"Form is no other than emptiness, emptiness no other than form." *Prajnaparamita* means literally "the wisdom that leads to the other shore," that
is, intuitive wisdom.

RINZAI GIGEN (Jap.; Ch., Lin-chi I-hsuan; ?-867): famed Chinese master
of the T'ANG period around whose teachings a special sect bearing his
name was formed. *Rinzai's Collected Sayings* (*Rinzairoku*) is a text widely
used by Rinzai masters in Japan. Rinzai is famous for his vivid speech
and forceful pedagogical methods.

ROSHI (Jap.): literally, "venerable teacher." Traditionally, training in Zen
is under a roshi, who may be a layman or a laywoman as well as a monk
or a priest. The function of a roshi is to guide and inspire disciples along
the path to Self-realization; a Zen teacher does not attempt directly to
control or influence their private lives. In olden days *roshi* was a hard-
won title, conferred by the public on one who had mastered the Buddha's DHARMA from the inside (which is to say through a direct experience of Truth), who had integrated it into his or her own life, and who
could lead others to this same experience. At a minimum it implied a
pure, steadfast character and a mature personality. To become a full-
fledged roshi demanded years of practice and study, full enlightenment,
and the seal of approval of one's own teacher, followed by years of ripen-

ing through "dharma dueling" with other masters. Nowadays the standards are less rigid, but the title *roshi*, if it is legitimately come by, is
still a title of distinction. Unfortunately, many in Japan today are ad-
dressed as *roshi* simply out of respect for their advanced age, and little
more. Masters in the true sense of the word are rare.

SADDHARMAPUNDARIKA-SUTRA (Skt.): the *Lotus Sutra*, a profound MAHA-
YANA text.

SAMADHI (Skt.): a term with a variety of meanings. In Zen it implies not
merely equilibrium, tranquility, and one-pointedness, but a state of intense yet effortless concentration, of complete absorption of the mind in
itself, of heightened and expanded awareness. *Samadhi* and *bodhi* are identical from the view of the enlightened BODHI-MIND. Seen from the developing stages leading to satori-awakening, however, samadhi and enlightenment are different.

SAMANTABHADRA AND MANJUSRI (Skt.; Jap., Fugen and Monju): BODHI-
SATTVAS. Bodhisattva Samantabhadra embodies calm action, compassion, and deep-seated wisdom. He is usually depicted astride a white
elephant (the elephant being noted for its tranquility and wisdom), sitting in attendance on the right side of the Buddha, while the Bodhisattva
Manjusri, with his delusion-cutting *vajra* (diamond) sword in one hand,
sits on the back of a lion on the Buddha's left. Manjusri represents awakening, that is, the sudden realization of the oneness of all existence and
the power arising therefrom, of which the lion's vigor is symbolic.
When the knowledge acquired through SATORI is employed for the benefit of humanity, Samantabhadra's compassion is manifesting itself. Accordingly, each of the bodhisattvas is an arm of the Buddha, represent-
ing, respectively, oneness (or equality) and manyness.

SAMSARA (Skt.): birth and death. The world of relativity; the transformation that all phenomena, including our thoughts and feelings, are cease-
lessly undergoing in accordance with the law of causation. Birth and
death can be compared to the waves on the ocean. The rise of a wave is
one "birth" and the fall is one "death." The size of each is conditioned
by the force of the previous one, itself being the progenitor of the suc-
ceeding wave. This process, infinitely repeated, is samsara.

SANGHA (Skt.): originally, the Buddhist monastic order, but more generally
the community of those who practice the Buddha's Way. The sangha is
one of the three treasures, or Jewels, of Buddhism, along with the Buddha and the DHARMA. See also THREE TREASURES.

S ATORI (Jap.): enlightenment, that is, Self-realization, opening the mind's eye, awakening to one's True Nature and hence the nature of all existence. See also KENSHO.

S ESSHIN (Jap.): literally, "to touch the mind"; a Zen retreat.

S HAKYAMUNI: see S IDDHARTHA G AUTAMA.

S HARIPUTRA: One of the great disciples of the Buddha.

S IDDHARTHA G AUTAMA: the historical Buddha. A prince born in northern India around 563 BCE, he left home at the age of twenty-nine, and after six years of arduous spiritual practice attained full enlightenment

and S UBHUTI: one of the foremost disciples of the Buddha. His questions and the Buddha's responses are the substance of the *Diamond Sutra*.

S URANGAMA-SUTRA (Skt.): a profound writing, originally in Sanskrit, widely venerated in all the M AHAYANA Buddhist countries. Among other topics, the SUTRA deals at length with the successive steps for the attainment of supreme enlightenment.

S UTRA (Skt.): literally, "thread on which jewels are strung." The sutras are the Buddhist scriptures, that is, the purported dialogues and sermons of Shakyamuni Buddha. There are said to be over ten thousand sutras, only a fraction of which have been translated into English. The so-called Hinayana were originally recorded in Pali, the M AHAYANA in Sanskrit. Most Buddhist sects are founded on one particular sutra from which they derive their authority—the Tendai and the Nichiren from the *Lotus Sutra*, the Kegon sect from the A VATAMSAKA-SUTRA, and so forth. Zen, however, is associated with no one sutra, and this gives the masters freedom to use the scriptures as and when they see fit or to ignore them entirely. In fact, Zen masters' attitude toward the sutras is not unlike that of skilled physicians toward drugs: they may prescribe one or more for a particular illness, or they may prescribe none. The familiar statement that Zen is a special transmission outside the scriptures, with no dependence on words and letters, only means that for the Zen sect, Truth must be directly grasped and not taken on the authority of even the sutras, much less sought in lifeless intellectual formulas or concepts. Still, most Japanese masters do not frown on sutra-reading after a disciple has attained KENSHO if it acts as a spur to full enlightenment.

T'ANG E RA: the period from 618 to 906 in ancient China that saw the magnificent flowering of the Zen tradition in all its vitality and genius.

T EISHO: Zen talk by a roshi that presents the DHARMA.

TEN THOUSAND THINGS: traditional Chinese Buddhist expression meaning all things, the tremendous variety of forms, immeasurable, beyond counting.

THREE TREASURES or JEWELS: All Buddhist religious life is rooted in faith in and reverence for the three treasures—Buddha, DHARMA, and SANGHA. The three treasures can be understood on various levels. Ultimately they are to be found in ourselves, aspects of our own profoundest nature.

TUSHITA HEAVENS: among the highest and purest heavens, where MAITREYA, the Buddha of the next world age, presently abides. There are many heavens as well as many hells in Buddhist cosmology.

UPAYA (Skt.): the "skillful means" by which DHARMA teachings are adapted to the needs of each person so as to be most effective in easing suffering and bringing about liberation.

VIMALAKIRTI (Skt.; Ch., Yuima; Jap., Yuimakitsu): the great layman of the Buddha's own time, said to have attained to the same level of spiritual development as the Buddha himself; the subject of the profound, and profoundly iconoclastic, *Vimalakirti-sutra*.

WAY: the Tao, the essence or truth of the universe; the way of Truth.

YAMA RAJA (Skt.): in Buddhist and Hindu mythology, the lord or judge of the dead before whom all who die must come for judgment. Yama Raja holds up the mirror of KARMA, wherein are reflected the good and evil deeds of the deceased, who then consign themselves either to a happy realm or, if their deeds have been preponderantly evil, to frightful tortures.

ZAZEN (Jap.): literally, "sitting Zen." Zazen is to be distinguished from meditation, which usually involves a visualization or putting into the mind a concept, an idea, or another thought-form. In zazen the mind empties of all random, extraneous thoughts and becomes one-pointed and stable. In this condition it can awaken to its own nature. Zazen is not limited to the sitting posture but can proceed throughout the activities of life.

ZENDO (Jap.): large hall or room—in large temples or centers, a separate structure—where ZAZEN is practiced.

Bibliography

KOAN COLLECTIONS

Aitken, Robert, trans. and ed. *The Gateless Barrier: The Wu-Men Kuan (Mumonkan).* New York: Farrar, Straus and Giroux, 1991.

Blyth, R. H. *Mumonkan.* Vol. 4 of *Zen and Zen Classics.* Tokyo: Hokuseido Press, 1966.

Cleary, Thomas, and J. C. Cleary, trans. *The Blue Cliff Record.* Boulder: Prajna Press, 1978.

Kapleau, Philip, ed. and comp. "The Hekiganroku." Rochester: The Rochester Zen Center, November 1984. Photocopy.

Kapleau, Philip, ed. and comp. "The Mumonkan." Rochester: The Rochester Zen Center, November 1991. Photocopy.

Sekida, Katsuki. *Two Zen Classics: Mumonkan and Hekiganroku, with Commentaries.* New York: Weatherhill, 1977.

Shibayama, Zenkei. *Zen Comments on the Mumonkan.* Trans. by Sumiko Kudo. New York: Harper and Row, 1974.

Yamada, Koun. *Gateless Gate.* Tucson: The University of Arizona Press, 1990.

SUTRAS

Cleary, Thomas, trans. *The Flower Ornament Scripture: A Translation of the Avatamsaka Sutra.* Boston: Shambhala, 1987.

Emmerick, R. E., trans. *The Khotanese Surangamasamadhisutra.* London: Oxford University Press, 1970.

Goddard, Dwight, ed. *A Buddhist Bible*. Boston: Beacon Press, 1994.

Kato, Bunno, Yoshiro Tamura, and Kojiro Miyasaka, trans. *The Threefold Lotus Sutra*. New York: Weatherhill, 1975.

Price, A. F., and Wong Mou-Lam, trans. *The Diamond Sutra and the Sutra of Hui-Neng*. Berkeley: Shambhala, 1969.

Robinson, Richard H., trans. "The Sutra of Vimalakirti's Preaching." Department of Indian Studies, University of Wisconsin, 1967. Photocopy.

Rochester Zen Center. "Master Hakuin's Chant in Praise of Zazen," in "Chants." Rochester: The Rochester Zen Center, 1990. Photocopy.

Rochester Zen Center. "Prajna Paramita Hridaya: Heart of Perfect Wisdom," in "Chants." Rochester: The Rochester Zen Center, 1990. Photocopy.

Thurman, Robert, trans. *The Holy Teaching of Vimalakirti: A Mahayana Scripture*. University Park: Pennsylvania State University Press, 1976.

Watson, Burton, trans. *The Vimalakirti Sutra*. New York: Columbia University Press, 1996.

Yampolsky, Philip B., trans. *The Platform Sutra of the Sixth Patriarch: The Text of the Tun-Huang Manuscript*. New York: Columbia University Press, 1967.

BACKGROUND MATERIAL

Cleary, Thomas, trans. *Rational Zen: The Mind of Dogen*. Boston: Shambhala, 1993.

Conze, Edward, trans. *Buddhist Scriptures*. New York: Penguin, 1959.

de Bary, Wm. Theodore. *The Buddhist Tradition in India, China and Japan*. New York: Random House/Modern Library, 1969.

Miura, Isshu, and Ruth Fuller Sasaki. *Zen Dust*. New York: Harcourt, Brace, and World, 1966.

Sasaki, Ruth Fuller, Yoshitaka Iriya, and Dana R. Fraser, trans. *A Man of Zen: The Recorded Sayings of Layman P'ang*. New York: Weatherhill, 1971.

Suzuki, D. T. *Manual of Zen Buddhism*. New York: Grove Press, 1960.

Watson, Burton, trans. *The Zen Teachings of Master Lin-Chi*. New York: Columbia University Press, 1999.

Wu, John C. H. *The Golden Age of Zen*. New York: Doubleday, 1996.

Zimmer, Heinrich. *Philosophies of India*. London: Routledge and Kegan Paul, 1969.

Works by Roshi Philip Kapleau

Awakening to Zen: The Teachings of Roshi Philip Kapleau. Edited by Polly Young-Eisendrath and Rafe Martin. New York: Scribner, 1997.

The Zen of Living and Dying: A Practical and Spiritual Guide. Boston: Shambhala, 1998.

The Three Pillars of Zen: Teaching, Practice, and Enlightenment (Thirty-Fifth Anniversary Edition). Updated and revised, with a new afterword. New York: Random House/Anchor, 2000.

Zen: Merging of East and West. New York: Random House/Anchor, 2000.

Books by Philip Kapleau

Straight to the Heart of Zen: Eleven Classic Koans and Their Inner Meanings

Koans are at the very heart of Zen practice; this collection of informal koan talks will bring the Zen student into the presence of Roshi Philip Kapleau, the author of *The Three Pillars of Zen*. The talks in this collection came directly from the *zendo* (training hall) and from the intense form of practice known as *sesshin*, a Japanese word meaning "to train the mind." These are direct presentations of the practice and understanding of one of the century's greatest American masters.

The Zen of Living and Dying: A Practical and Spiritual Guide

To live life fully and die serenely—surely we all share these goals, so inextricably entwined. Yet a spiritual dimension is too often lacking in the attitudes, circumstances, and rites of death in modern society. Kapleau explores the subject of death and dying on a deeply personal level, interweaving the writings of Western religions with insights from his own Zen practice, and offers practical advice for the dying and their families.